REPAIR & RENOVATE

floors&stairs

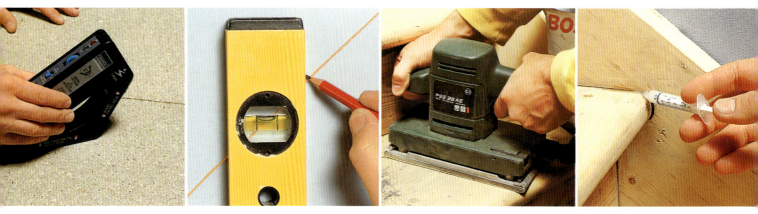

REPAIR & RENOVATE

floors&stairs

Mark Corke

MURDOCH BOOKS

690.1
1455984

floors & stairs contents

*Recent years have seen a revival of interest in vinyl tiles,
which are now available in a variety of colours and styles.*

Balusters are not nailed in place but are fitted between the handrail and stringing by means of spacing blocks.

introduction

Home improvement is fast becoming a national pastime, with more and more enthusiasts choosing to undertake jobs that used to be left to professional tradespeople. Taking on a project yourself and seeing it through from planning to final decoration can be more rewarding than hiring someone else and helps to ensure you achieve the desired look – and with minimal labour costs there are real savings to be made.

considering renovations

Few things give as much satisfaction as owning a home, and for many people using their own DIY skills to create the ideal living environment for themselves and their family is part of the enjoyment. Even after the decoration and renovation is complete there are always odd jobs to be done over the years to cope with inevitable wear and tear. Increasing numbers of people are finding out how rewarding DIY can be, and what was once seen as a chore or only work that could be entrusted to a professional is now regarded as a creative and worthwhile pastime.

In this book you will encounter repair and renovation projects ranging from the straightforward and simple to advanced and complex construction projects. Unless you are certain of your abilities it is probably best not to start immediately on one of the more difficult projects. If you are a newcomer to DIY then starting on one of the smaller jobs, which can easily be completed in a day or weekend, will help build your confidence and develop basic skills that can be applied to the more ambitious, long-term projects elsewhere in this book. Nothing is more demoralizing at first than starting a project above your skill level, which drags on week after week. If you do not actually enjoy doing the project then you will not be giving it your best attention and more than likely you will end up with a second-rate job.

Any repair or renovation project will cost money, so when planning the work you should have a firm idea at an early stage how much everything will cost and how much you are

BELOW *Solid wood floors can be expensive and difficult to lay, but laying laminate flooring is a much simpler DIY task and the finished result can look equally stunning in the right setting.*

willing to spend. Make an estimate of the likely expense and be prepared for one or two unexpected hidden costs as well – even professional builders have a contingency fund. Consider also the work that is best left to a professional, in particular you may decide to leave the plumbing and electrical work to a qualified person. Even if you have the necessary skills and experience to undertake this work yourself, it is wise to employ a professional to check over your handiwork to ensure it has been correctly carried out and, above all, that there are no safety concerns.

You may already have ideas about renovations and improvements that you would like to make to your home, but before getting out the tools and rushing to begin in

RIGHT *A dark stained hardwood staircase helps to make this entrance hall look warm and inviting, whilst the ornamental balusters and newel posts create a sense of grandeur.*

BELOW *If space is restricted where a staircase is to be installed, by dividing it into two flights at right angles to each other the stairs will fit without needing to be too steep.*

earnest, it is strongly recommended that you read all the way through this book. Not only will it help you to identify problems that you might have overlooked, but it may also provide further ideas to make the best of your home.

We use floors and stairs every day but all too often when redecorating very little thought is given to the flooring or stairway. Yet the floor covering in a room has a crucial influence on its appearance, while stairs are one of the strongest architectural elements in a house.

Throughout this book you will see safety boxes giving advice and sensible precautions. Take heed of these and your projects will be safe and fun. As long as you read and understand each of the sections in this book, the repair and renovation projects you carry out should provide you with the satisfaction of a job well done and help you to get the most enjoyment out of your home.

RIGHT *Impermeable and easily wiped, vinyl is ideal for use in a bathroom and is available in sheet form or tiles.*

BELOW *Quarry tiles offer the ultimate in durability and laying them yourself can save a lot of money.*

The layout of this book has been designed to provide project instruction in as comprehensive yet straightforward a manner as possible. The sample page featured below provides a guideline to the different elements incorporated into the page design and indicates how best to make use of them. Full colour photos and diagrams combined with explanatory text, laid out in a clear, step-by-step order, provide easy-to-follow instructions. Each project is prefaced by a blue box containing a list of tools so that you will know in advance the range of equipment required for the job. Other boxes of additional text accompany each project, which are aimed at drawing your attention to particular issues. Pink safety boxes alert the reader to issues of safety and detail any precautions that may need to be taken. They also indicate where a particular job must be carried out by a tradesperson. Green tip boxes offer professional hints for the best way to go about a particular task involved in the project. Boxes with an orange border describe alternative options and techniques, which are relevant to the project in hand but not demonstrated on the page.

difficulty rating

The following symbols are designed to give an indication of difficulty level relating to particular tasks and projects in this book. Clearly what are simple jobs to one person may be difficult to another, and vice versa. These guidelines are primarily based on the ability of an individual in relation to the experience and degree of technical ability required.

Straightforward and requires limited technical skills

Straightforward but requires a reasonable skill level

Technically quite difficult, and could involve a number of skills

High skill level required and involves a number of techniques

safety boxes, coloured pink for emphasis, draw attention to the safety considerations for each project

tip boxes provide helpful hints, developed from experience, on the best way to achieve particular tasks

a list of tools is given at the beginning of each project

options boxes offer additional instruction on techniques related to the project in hand

colour-coordinated tabs help you quickly find your place again when moving between chapters

anatomy of floors & stairs

Floors and stairs are used every day with little thought given to how they are constructed. To some degree their design will be determined by the building codes and regulations in force at the time the house was built and the materials that were available. Within these parameters, however, there is substantial scope for variation in construction to satisfy different purposes and functions, while the preferences of the architect and the relationship of the building to its surroundings will also have an impact. The following chapter identifies and examines the main types of floor and stair construction.

Spiral stairs are built up one unit at a time, with each unit comprising a single tread attached to a section of the central post.

concrete floor construction

Most people think of concrete floors as having a rather industrial feel and consider them second-rate compared to a traditional suspended timber floor, so that they should only really be used for basements or garages. Yet concrete has many advantages and now more than ever before concrete floors are being laid for the main living areas in homes. In particular they are perfect for heavy load-bearing applications and provide an ideal subfloor for many types of floor covering.

concrete floors

Concrete floors can fulfil several different functions. If the house is built on a concrete raft then the ground floor will form part of this foundation and will be part of the overall structure of the property. Concrete floors often form part of a slab that supports walls for the upper storeys, while at the same time providing a smooth level subfloor over which a screed is often laid. If a timber floor has been stripped out and replaced with concrete then this will not obviously have any structural reference to the house. Concrete is most often used at ground level, although it is not unheard of to find concrete floors at higher levels.

When laid correctly concrete has an almost indefinite life span making it a cost-effective replacement for a rotten ground floor. Some older concrete floors can be damp but this is often due to defective damp-proofing and not directly due to the breakdown of the concrete. Newly laid concrete must be allowed to dry out before any flooring material may be fitted. This will take anything from three weeks to several months, depending upon the thickness of the screed.

Concrete serves as an excellent subfloor for many different floor coverings. It is not subject to movement like timber and is capable of handling heavy loads, making it suitable for kitchens and utility rooms where heavy appliances might otherwise damage a timber floor.

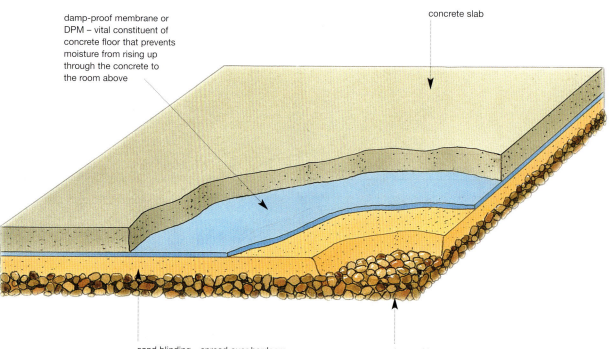

damp-proof membrane or DPM – vital constituent of concrete floor that prevents moisture from rising up through the concrete to the room above

concrete slab

sand blinding – spread over hardcore layer so the damp-proof membrane is not torn by the rubble

layer of hardcore – this builds up the level and provides a stable base for the concrete

Concrete is a mixture of coarse and fine aggregates – stones up to around 20mm (¾in) in diameter with smaller stones and coarse sand – that is bound together into a solid matrix by cement. You can buy the ingredients separately from builders' suppliers and mix them yourself, buy dry ready-mixed bags of cement and aggregate (ideal for small jobs) or order ready-mixed concrete (best for large areas).

Ready-mixed concrete may be delivered by a large truck mixer with its familiar slowly turning drum, or by a smaller vehicle that carries dry cement, aggregates plus a cement mixer and can mix the amount you need on the spot. Truck mixers can deliver up to about 6cu m (200cu ft) of concrete from their chutes directly to the site. Smaller vehicles mix by the barrowload, which you then have to move from truck to site.

The ingredients of a concrete mix depend on the use to which the material will be put. The ideal mix for laying a concrete floor is 1 part ordinary Portland cement, 1 part building sand and 3 parts aggregate. All-in aggregate is a mixture of sharp sand and 20mm (¾in) aggregate. Always mix ingredients by volume, using separate buckets or similar containers of the same size for cement and aggregate. Mix batches based on 1 bucket of cement plus the relevant numbers of buckets of sand and aggregate. Be careful when mixing not to splash cement on your skin and eyes – wash it off immediately if you do.

tools for the job

mixing board
shovel
clean bucket
wheelbarrow
hired cement mixer

by hand

Measure out the sand and aggregate into a compact heap. Form a crater in the centre with a shovel and add the cement. Mix the ingredients dry until the pile is uniform in colour and texture. If you are using dry ready-mixed concrete, tip out the sack and mix thoroughly. Form a crater in the centre of the heap and add water.

The aggregate will contain some water already, so the amount you need to add will be trial and error to begin with. After two or three batches, you will be better able to gauge how much to add. Turn dry material from the edge of the heap into the central crater. Keep on mixing and adding a little more water in turn until the mix reaches the right consistency – it should retain ridges formed in it with the shovel. If it is too sloppy, add dry ingredients, correctly proportioned as before, to stiffen it up again.

with a mixer

If you are using a cement mixer, set it up on its stand and check that it is secure. Put some aggregate and water in the drum and start it turning.

Add most of the cement and sand, then water and solid material alternately, to ensure thorough mixing. Run the mixer for two minutes once all the ingredients are in, then tip out some of the contents into a wheelbarrow. The mix should fall cleanly off the mixer blades.

COLOURING CONCRETE

Special paints made specifically for colouring concrete can be applied once the floor has been poured and allowed to cure, or pigments can be added to wet concrete while it is being mixed. The advantage of using pigments is that they are longer-lasting and the concrete will retain its colour regardless of wear on the floor.

timber floor construction

In the vast majority of homes the floors will be constructed from timber. Until quite recently a timber floor meant just that – a floor constructed out of solid wood floorboards nailed on top of solid wood joists. However, technological advances have altered many of the traditional methods of construction so that chipboard and plyboard are commonly used instead of timber. The age of the property will have a bearing on the method of construction, with newer houses tending to make use of sheet flooring, which provides a smooth base over which to lay a floor covering.

traditional timber floor

The diagram below illustrates the traditional method of constructing a timber floor. Floorboards may be either square-edged or joined to each other with the aid of a tongue and groove joint, which helps to cut down on draughts. New houses tend not to have floorboards as it is a much slower and more expensive process to lay floorboards than laying sheet flooring. Where renovations have taken place quite often you will find that floorboards have been ripped out and chipboard sheets laid instead, although recently there has been a vogue for plain, exposed floorboards in interior design. Where an upper storey floor has been constructed using this traditional method, it is likely that the ceiling below will follow the old-style lath and plaster construction.

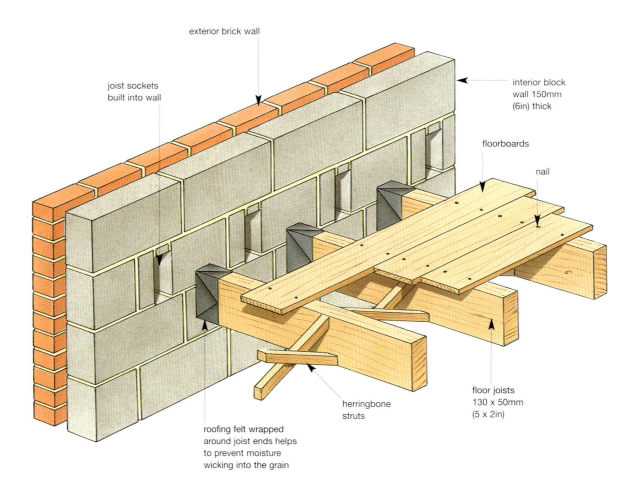

exterior brick wall

joist sockets
built into wall

interior block
wall 150mm
(6in) thick

floorboards

nail

floor joists
130 x 50mm
(5 x 2in)

herringbone
struts

roofing felt wrapped
around joist ends helps
to prevent moisture
wicking into the grain

Suspended floors in modern houses are commonly supported by joist hangers. These prevent the timber joists from coming into direct contact with the brickwork or blockwork, so that moisture cannot wick into the ends of the joists. The joists will often be thinner than those used in traditional construction, and sheet chipboard in place of floorboards acts as a stressed component tying everything together. Where the floor forms a ceiling for the room below this will be of plasterboard skimmed with a plaster finish.

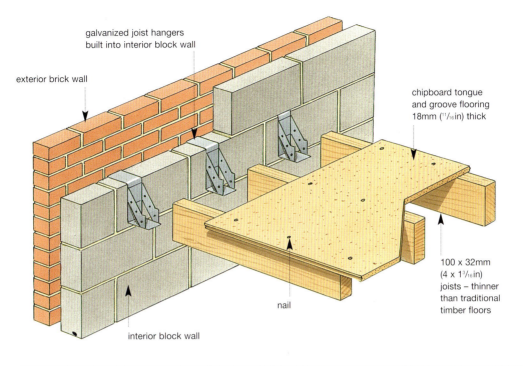

galvanized joist hangers built into interior block wall

exterior brick wall

chipboard tongue and groove flooring 18mm (¹¹/₁₆in) thick

100 x 32mm (4 x 1³/₁₆in) joists – thinner than traditional timber floors

nail

interior block wall

This type of floor is found in houses that utilize timber framing for structural walls and is common in the USA. It may look inferior but in actual fact 'I' beam construction is extremely strong and stiff. The beams can be made on site but are most often manufactured under controlled conditions and bought in. As with floors supported by joist hangers, sheet materials will usually be employed as flooring and ceiling for beam floors.

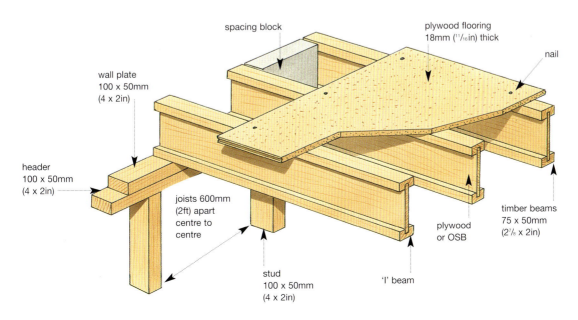

spacing block

plywood flooring 18mm (¹¹/₁₆in) thick

nail

wall plate 100 x 50mm (4 x 2in)

header 100 x 50mm (4 x 2in)

joists 600mm (2ft) apart centre to centre

stud 100 x 50mm (4 x 2in)

'I' beam

plywood or OSB

timber beams 75 x 50mm (2⁷/₈ x 2in)

stair construction

When you enter a house the staircase will quite often be the first thing you see, leading up from the hallway to the first floor landing. A staircase is thus always 'on show' and its shape and design can influence greatly the look and feel of an interior. The shape and position of the stairs will largely be determined by the structure of the house, but variations in the style of balustrades and handrails and the materials from which they are constructed provide opportunities for altering appearance. Most stairs in homes are made from timber but concrete and metal are not uncommon.

traditional stairs

The diagram below illustrates the style and method of construction of a traditional timber staircase. By far the majority of homes will include this type of staircase, though naturally other types may be encountered. Lengths of wood called strings form the sides of the stairs, which may be cut from either solid timber or MDF (medium-density fibreboard). These strings have zigzag housings trenched into them, into which risers and tread boards are then glued. When properly constructed and finished, such stairs will give years of trouble-free service.

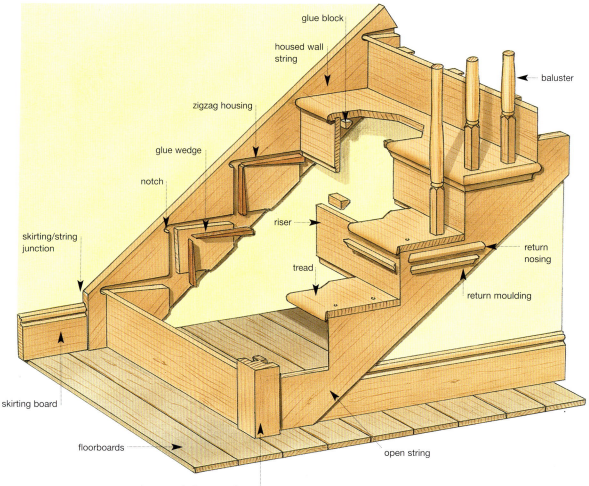

Concrete stairs are comparatively rare in residential properties but by no means unknown. They can be built off site or on the job, but will take more time to construct and are substantially heavier than their timber counterparts. Where a house is constructed on a sloping site they may be used outside the front or back door. The look of the concrete may be softened by adding brick facings, or it is possible to add a decorative coat of paint.

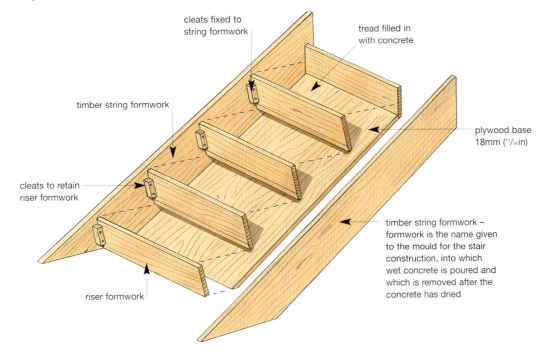

cleats fixed to string formwork

tread filled in with concrete

timber string formwork

plywood base 18mm ($1^{1}/_{16}$in)

cleats to retain riser formwork

timber string formwork – formwork is the name given to the mould for the stair construction, into which wet concrete is poured and which is removed after the concrete has dried

riser formwork

spiral stairs

Spiral stairs represent an unusual option for fitting a staircase, and are often chosen purely for style to create a 'retro' focal point in the house. However, they are also a highly effective choice where space is at a premium. Spiral stairs can be made from wood, metal, concrete or a combination of all these materials. As you would expect, spiral stairs are more difficult to build than either a concrete or traditional timber staircase. The diagram on the right illustrates the most common mode of construction, whereby timber or cast iron sections are jointed or bolted together on site. Although pleasing to the eye, the twist in spiral staircases can make moving furniture difficult, especially when the outside edge of the stairs is bound by a wall.

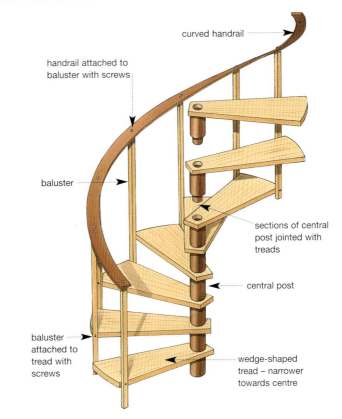

curved handrail

handrail attached to baluster with screws

baluster

baluster attached to tread with screws

sections of central post jointed with treads

central post

wedge-shaped tread – narrower towards centre

planning

Once you have decided to undertake a DIY project there is a huge temptation to jump straight in and get started, dealing with any necessary preparations as you encounter them. However, careful and lengthy planning before any work is begun should never be seen as a waste of time, but instead should be regarded as an integral part of the job. Proper thought will save time and tempers later on, allow the work to progress more smoothly and could reduce the costs in the long run. One of the most important issues you need to consider at this planning stage is whether you intend to carry out all the work yourself or will need to hire professionals. Official planning approval may also be required, so you should consult your local authority at this stage and certainly before work commences. Other key questions you need to ask yourself are whether you have the tools, materials, funds, experience and commitment needed to see the work through?

The combination of steel and timber in this short flight of stairs contributes to the contemporary industrial feel to the interior.

options for change

Floors and stairs are key structural and decorative features in a property and making changes in these areas can have a major impact on the overall appearance of your home. However, when planning changes you should consider carefully any original and period features that it would be better to retain. For example, things that will have attracted you to the property in the first place should be preserved. It is all too easy to over-modernize or renovate the original features out of existence. Remember that whilst you are doing this work for your own pleasure and enjoyment of the property you may well be wanting to sell it in the future.

flooring options

There are now probably more choices when it comes to flooring than there have ever been. Wall-to-wall carpeting has traditionally been the first choice for many people, both because it is soft underfoot and also because it provides additional insulation to any room, helping to create a cosy and inviting home environment. However, a good carpet can be expensive and may not be the best choice for high traffic areas or damp rooms such as bathrooms and kitchens. In these areas harder flooring materials will be better suited and many of these can be laid to a professional finish by a DIY enthusiast with only modest skills. Quarry tiles are becoming an increasingly popular

RIGHT *A wooden or timber laminate floor can be an excellent choice of flooring for a teenager's bedroom.*

hard tile option, and although expensive they will add value to almost any home. Vinyl sheet flooring has enjoyed continuous popularity since its introduction, with an ever increasing range of styles and colours now available. Timber laminate flooring has seen a recent vogue and provides a tough surface that is relatively easy to lay and maintain. If you are fortunate enough to have well-maintained floorboards, then it is possible to stain, varnish or paint your floorboards for an entirely new look with minimum capital outlay. Whilst not strictly part of the floor itself a well chosen moulding or skirting will complement the flooring. Many newly built homes have rather small skirting boards with little or no decorative moulding. Changing this to match a laminate floor or picking out one of the colours in the floor covering is a simple but effective way to enhance the look of the flooring.

LEFT *Quarry tiles are unsurpassed when it comes to durability and are ideal for rooms that open onto outdoor areas.*

stairs & landing options

Stairs too can be made to look completely different by often the cheapest and simplest of treatments. By making a few repairs, stripping the existing finish and applying a new finish such as stain or paint, an old staircase can often be completely rejuvenated – dark brown Victorian stairs will brighten up a treat with a few coats of stain or paint. A relatively easy way of altering the structure of a staircase, and opening up the stairway more to the rest of the house, is to replace solid handrail panelling with open balusters. Many of the large DIY stores are now offering a range of stair components such as balusters, handrails and newels which can be installed by anyone with moderate skills to transform the look of a plain staircase. The landing too will benefit from the same treatment as the stairs and should always be considered in the overall scheme of stair renovation. For example, by continuing a balustrade along the upstairs landing you will ensure a unified look.

ABOVE RIGHT *Turned spindles, balusters and curved handrails give this staircase an air of classical elegance, blending traditional style with a modern use of materials.*

MIDDLE RIGHT *Stairs need not be made entirely of wood – a mix of materials can create stylish effects and a metal balustrade such as this also helps to save space.*

BELOW *A window opening at the bottom of the stairwell helps to lighten and open up this compact staircase, although it is important to install plenty of artificial light fittings as well.*

loft stairways

Foldaway loft or attic ladders are cheap and easy to install but are not stairways in the true sense. If the loft is to be used as a bedroom or other habitable room as defined in the building regulations, then a stronger and more permanent form of stairs will have to be installed. If at first it seems impossible to accommodate a stairway up to the loft, do not lose heart. Instead, seek professional advice and you will be surprised just what is possible. If the details on a new stairway are made to match the main staircase, then it will become part of the overall structure of the house and will not look out of place or like a recent addition.

planning the work

Even if you are just completing a job that will only take a few hours at the weekend, it is well worth planning out the order of work before starting. Getting halfway through a project only to find that you have run out of some basic material is not only annoying but may also ruin the job in hand so that you need to start again. Any work on your home will inevitably cause some disruption. By working out a plan you will at least have an idea of how long this is likely to last and perhaps be able make some alternative arrangements. The following factors must be taken into account when planning the order of work.

making time

One of the advantages of carrying out home improvements yourself is that, unlike a professional builder, you will not have to work out an hourly rate for your time, but you should still consider carefully how you order your own time.

- Be realistic about the timescale taken to do the job, and do not set unattainable targets and unrealistic deadlines. Far better to add on an additional day than to rush and end up with a sub-standard job.

- Setting aside a lengthy block of time means that you will not be interrupting your flow of work. If you have some surplus paid holiday from your job, you will probably find that by tacking an extra day or two onto the end of a weekend the job can be completed in one go rather than being stretched over several weekends – picking up where you left off from the day before, rather than from the previous weekend, is always easier. Many items of hired equipment are booked up weeks in advance at weekends but are little used during weekdays, so you may also find that you can get hold of these sooner.

- If you need to factor tradespeople into the schedule, you will have to estimate your time accurately so that you can get professional help in at the correct time. Having a plumber turn up to connect the bath when you have yet to fit the floor might not only be embarrassing but you could be charged for a wasted trip. Involve any professionals at an early stage as they are likely to be booked up weeks in advance.

- Above all be flexible and be prepared to amend your plans if you discover something that needs attention. Older houses in particular can throw up nasty surprises at times.

sequence of jobs

- Work to a sequence so that any major jobs that may impact on future work are completed first. For example, if the roof is leaking or there is a dripping tap in the bathroom, you should fix these two items first before you lay the floor covering, otherwise the new floor could suffer from damp problems and you could quickly find yourself having to replace it again; or if the house needs rewiring then it is better to get this done before you think about laying new carpets.

- If you are renovating several rooms in your house consider how work in one room might impact on another. For example, if you need to access one room from another then wait till the end of the project to decorate both rooms. Do not make the mistake of laying an expensive floor if you know that you will have to walk across it in muddy boots to access the next room.

tools and materials

- Ensure you have all the necessary tools and materials before starting work. You should be able to buy most tools off the shelf, but some heavy-duty tools may need to be ordered. Before rushing out to buy expensive equipment, work out which tools will get repeated use and which are for one-off jobs, as it is probably more cost-effective to hire tools in the latter category rather than buying outright.

- If you are intending to hire heavy-duty equipment, such as a concrete mixer or an electric sander, reserve this well in advance so that you will have it to hand at the correct time during the project.

- If you need to order materials, such as laminate flooring or carpets, there can often be a delay of several weeks between order and delivery, which will need to accounted for in your schedule.

- Make sure you know the dimensions of whatever solid materials you will be using – timber, tiles, plasterboard, plywood and the like – and use these as units to count the required quantities.

- With bagged and loose materials such as cement, sand and plaster, find out the coverage per bag and use this to work out how many bags you will need.

- Do not be tempted to overestimate – it is wasteful to go beyond a sensible safety margin of, say, 5 per cent. Conversely do not underestimate as this is annoying if you run out of something just as the shops are closing.

extras

- Waste disposal is a job that is often overlooked but must also be accounted for in the schedule of work, for example you may need to hire a skip to take away old flooring or construction materials.

- Include extra time for general finishing and room decoration, if required.

- If you need to apply for planning consent you must allow eight weeks from submission until you receive a decision. Finding out if you need to file an application and submitting this should form part of your preparations.

Careful planning down to the last detail is the key to a successful, stress-free job.

SCALE DRAWINGS

Making a scale drawing of the room on graph paper will help to estimate quantities and serve to remind you of what you need when visiting stores and suppliers. Such drawings need not be of an architect's standard, but they should offer enough detail to provide a good idea of the effect a project will have on the existing look of your home. Graph paper always makes any technical drawing easier and allows for more accurate measurement. Mark on the positions of the doors and windows and any other permanent fixtures, then add furniture to the diagram so that you can gauge the effect of the alteration on the overall layout of the room.

dealing with professionals

Whilst it is true that almost any DIY project is possible for a skilled amateur, there are times when it pays to employ professionals. It may be that you are completing one or more of the jobs in this book as part of a much larger renovation or conversion project, and although you feel capable of laying a new floor covering you maybe do not have the time or confidence to construct a whole new staircase from scratch. Or it could be that you would simply like architectural drawings prepared. Whatever you need the secret is to find reliable professional help at the right price.

choosing a tradesperson

- Always try and get a personal recommendation by asking around friends. If you walk or drive past a house where some work has just been completed, do not be afraid to approach the owners to find out whether they were pleased with the work and would recommend the builders again.

- If you cannot get a recommendation another option is to look through your local yellow pages. You will find there are literally hundreds of builders who all want your business. Look for those who are members of a recognized trade association such as the Federation of Master Builders. To belong to this organization the builder must supply references along with proof of adequate insurance cover.

- Bear in mind that a good builder will be booked up for weeks, if not months, in advance and they should be approached well in advance of when you would like work to begin.

- Having produced a list of prospective contractors who are willing and able to do the job, now is the time to 'shop around' asking for estimates from each builder. Write down your specification and give this to each one to ensure that they are quoting on a like-for-like basis.

- When the contractors offer their estimates do not necessarily opt for the cheapest but rather go for the best all-round deal. You may find that the least expensive has omitted certain costs, which will inevitably surface at the quotation stage. The best estimate is likely to be the most detailed, where the costs have been broken down and each one can be justified.

- Look at other work that your prospective contractors have undertaken. Do not be scared to do this, if they are a reputable firm they will be pleased to show you.

- **Architects** – These skilled professionals can be worth employing if you are undertaking large or complex alterations. They can prepare all the technical drawings for you, deal with the local authority, apply for any necessary permission and, if the job is extensive, can supervise the contractors or sub-contractors. Architects practising in the UK must be members of the RIBA (Royal Institute of British Architects) from whom you can obtain the names of architects in you area.

- **Surveyors** – These people are skilled in evaluating the structural integrity of buildings. If you hire a surveyor because you are concerned about the structural condition of your property, their survey might typically cover such things as rot and infestation, whether there is any presence of damp in the building, the condition of the plumbing and other services, and the overall condition of the property. They will inspect your home and may make recommendations as to what work they feel is necessary. For instance, if your floor is sagging in the front room, they may suggest that the floor should be replaced and will also able to tell you what caused the problems and the best way to prevent a recurrence.

If you are intending to hire professionals to carry out major construction work on your home, it is vital to ensure that you pick a competent and reputable individual or firm and that a detailed costing and timescale are agreed upon in advance.

negotiating a price

- An estimate is merely an indication of what the final cost is likely to be and can be in the form of a written or verbal estimate. An estimate is not a formal contract.

- A quotation is a fixed price and will be the price that you pay. The figure is legally binding and forms the basis of the contract made between you and the professional. Any variation or changes on either side should be agreed in writing between the two parties. When looking at the cost for work to be carried out, the figure should not change unless you alter specifications for the work.

- Never offer to pay tradespeople up front, as this can encourage them to neglect the project – if money is to be paid once work is completed this is a greater incentive for them to stay on site.

- If expensive materials need to be bought, however, it is acceptable for the tradesperson to expect that these costs will be met prior to installation.

- Give clear instructions and specifications for any work. Outline precisely what you are asking the contractor to do and what is to be done by others. This avoids misunderstandings and disputes later on.

- Payments should be agreed at an early stage and certainly before work starts. For larger contracts likely to take some time, such as a major house extension, you will need to agree a schedule indicating stages when payment will be made for a specific portion of work. There are times when payments should be withheld, but on the other hand unnecessary delays will sour relationships. If the contractor has done a good job then they should be paid promptly, certainly within their terms of payment.

rules & regulations

Most minor repairs and interior decoration are not subject to any specific rules and regulations with the force of law, although you should follow your own self-imposed rules concerning safe practice and sound construction. Areas where you will need to conform with legal standards and follow the correct procedures for gaining approval are those which involve major building work and/or alteration to the external appearance or structure of the building. Most alterations to floors and stairs will not require planning permission, but it is best to check before starting or you may have to undo all your hard work. Any major construction, including laying floors and altering staircases, is subject to building regulations enforced by local authorities.

planning permission

The phrase 'planning permission' refers to the legal permission that needs to be sought from a local authority before any significant alterations to the structure of a property may be undertaken. Although it is unlikely that you will need to seek planning permission for most alterations to floors and stairs, you do need to be aware of your responsibility under the planning regulations. The following short guide will help you assess whether you need to apply for planning permission, how to go about it and what is entailed in the process:

- Planning rules and regulations are designed to ensure that any new building or alterations to existing buildings are suitable for the surrounding area and will not impact adversely on neighbouring properties.

- You are generally free to carry out renovation projects in the home without planning permission, although there are exceptions, especially where major changes are involved. For example, the installation of an additional stairway to an attic as part of a conversion project designed to create more living accommodation may fall into this category. If your home is in a conservation area or on the listed building register, you are much more likely to need planning permission for even minor alterations.

- All local authorities have planning officers who are responsible for overseeing the running and implementation of planning regulations. Your local planning officer will be able to inform you whether any work you intend to carry out will require planning consent.

- Many authorities publish booklets detailing the ins and outs of planning regulations and these may prove helpful in determining whether you require approval. Such booklets should be available free of charge from local libraries.

- Where planning consent is required you will need to pay a fee and submit plans, which you must file with the local authority along with an application form.

- You can submit the application yourself or you might prefer to employ an architect or architectural technician for this job. The advantage of doing this is that they are familiar with the process, know what is required and will be able to prepare any necessary drawings.

- Once the application has been made, by law the local authority must give you a decision within 8 weeks. You must not start any work until your application has been approved or you risk penalties.

- Planning consent is valid for 5 years – if you do not start the work within this time then you will have to make another application.

tips of the trade

When you speak to an officer at your local council they will be unfamiliar with your property. Take a few pictures of the building, in particular of the areas that you want to alter, and bring these along to the meeting. With this visual aid it will be easier to understand what the job entails and so a decision whether or not approval is required will be reached more quickly.

RIGHT *A Building Control Officer will visit the site of major construction to ensure all regulations are being adhered to.*

building regulations

Building regulations are concerned with local and national building codes and specify essential requirements that must be complied with. Any major alterations to your home will be subject to building regulations and significant alterations to a staircase or the replacement of a floor would fall into this category.

- A Building Control Officer (BCO) employed by the local authority has responsibility for enforcing building regulations. If you are planning any structural changes to your home then you will need to make an appointment with the BCO at the planning stages to discuss your ideas.

- As well as checking that your plans conform to regulations, BCOs can also be consulted on the project in general, so you should not be afraid to ask their advice. Although they cannot recommend a builder they may offer one or two ideas that you could incorporate into your scheme.

- If you are employing a professional builder it will normally be their responsibility to ascertain whether approval is required for whatever job they are undertaking and, if so, to gain permission before work commences.

- Once work has started it is more than likely that the BCO will visit the site to ensure that everything is being carried out in accordance with the necessary regulations.

- If the project is particularly extensive the BCO will need to visit the site at specific phases of the project. It is your responsibility to notify the BCO at the correct time.

- Once the job is finished the BCO will then sign a completion certificate to certify that the work has been carried out in accordance with building regulations.

- If any work contravenes building regulations or planning laws you could be faced with a large bill to put things right. Worse still you could be forced to reinstate the building to its original condition.

- You need not be daunted by all these regulations – get in touch with your local planning office and ask their advice. They would much rather be contacted at an early stage as this could save work on both sides.

tools & equipment

A basic tool kit is essential for home improvement work. At first the range of available tools can be bewildering but in reality much can be accomplished with just a few basic, good quality tools. As your skill and confidence grows you may find yourself wanting to purchase more specialized items. Money spent in this way is seldom wasted since good quality tools will last a lifetime.

general tools

A kit that includes the tools shown on this page will be sufficient to complete many of the projects in this book and most other general maintenance tasks around the home. Always buy the best tools you can afford and only add to the tool kit if you are certain the purchase will pay for itself in terms of time saved and ease of use.

claw hammer

bradawl

nail punch

pipe, joist and cable detector

slot-head screwdrivers

cross head screwdrivers

club hammer

insulated sleeves

bolster chisel

combination pliers

side cutters

long-nose pliers

half-round rasp

general purpose chisels

cordless drill/driver

mini level

carpenter's pencil

tape measure

sealant dispenser

stepladder

clamp

combination square

hacksaw

panel saw

pointing trowel

plastic bucket

trimming knife

workbench

mitresaw

For heavy-duty construction some specialist 'builder's' tools will be needed. Try to buy the finest quality tools as these will last longer, be easier to use and give the best results. Most of these tools can be bought from a good tool shop or builder's supply store – DIY stores may have a more limited range.

laser level

knee kicker

chalk line

sliding bevel

pincers

shovel

prybar

plastering trowel

mitre square

downward cutting jigsaw blade

vinyl roller

rout-a-bout and access hatch cutting attachment

floorboard jack

punner

carpenter's square

HIRING TOOLS

For isolated tasks that may require particularly heavy-duty equipment, or tools that are very expensive to buy, hiring is often the best option. This area has become a growing sector of the DIY market, and hire shops are increasingly catering for home repair enthusiasts as well as more traditional trade customers.

power tools

A cordless drill/driver has become an essential part of any tool kit and other power tools are growing in popularity due to their time-saving capabilities and competitive pricing.

Try not to buy either the cheapest or the most heavy-duty professional tools, but instead aim for somewhere between the two. It is possible to buy drill attachments for sanding, sawing and numerous other tasks. However, these are usually inferior to stand alone tools and the time spent constantly changing attachments can be frustrating.

power drill

jigsaw

router

electric sander

hiring specialist equipment

Certain projects described in this book will require the use of specialist tools and equipment, which are often large and expensive. If the equipment is only needed for the occasional job or one specific task it can be uneconomic to purchase it outright. Hiring a piece of equipment for a week, a day or just a few hours is a viable alternative and the market now widely caters for this growing practice amongst DIYers. Knowing that you have access to an almost unlimited range of specialist equipment will allow you to plan far more ambitious projects.

when to hire

When planning any job, however large or small, thought should be given to which skills and tools will be needed. In many cases the projects shown in this book can be completed successfully with a basic set of household tools. As your skill levels increase with experience and confidence, you will be amazed at just what can be achieved without recourse to a vast armoury of tools, but at times this is just not enough and a particular task will call for the aid of a specific piece of equipment. Just about any tool can be hired these days but it can be difficult for the amateur to know what is available and recognize when a piece of equipment is a candidate for hiring. Throughout this book you will see references to different tools. A basic tool kit is anatomized on page 28, which is sufficient to complete the majority of projects. Where larger pieces of machinery are

RIGHT *A small-scale concrete mixer can be hired for relatively little cost and will greatly contribute towards a professional finish.*

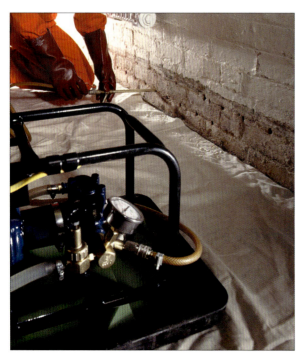

shown then it is safe to assume that these can be hired. That said, if you will be using such equipment for an extended period of time, or on a frequent basis, you should consider buying, as there may come a time when the total cost of the hire will be greater than the price tag of the tool.

what to hire

Equipment such as carpet cleaners are popular hire items, but there are plenty of others of which the average person may be unaware. Concrete mixers and floor sanders speed up the work magnificently, putting professional results within reach of the amateur. A small compressor and nail gun can be used to fix a large amount of floorboards down very quickly, whilst a powerfloat will give a smooth, glass-like finish to concrete and screeds.

LEFT *Although this damp-proof fluid injection machine is highly specialized, it is possible to hire one to do the job yourself.*

Once the preserve of the professional builder, hire shops are increasingly catering for the DIY market, and many stores even offer a home-delivery service at little extra charge for tools too big or too bulky to transport yourself. Before you start using an unfamiliar machine for the first time, it is vital that you fully understand how it operates, so make sure you have this explained to you before leaving the shop. Do not be afraid to ask for a demonstration if you are at all unsure. Staff in hire shops are usually very knowledgeable so do not be afraid to ask for advice. Often they will be able to suggest different methods for completing a task and direct you to tools that you might not know. Explain to them clearly what your project is, what tools you have already and what tools they would suggest you need to hire to complete the job. Many stores will have a catalogue, although do not expect this to explain how each piece of equipment works. It is more likely to give details of cost, minimum periods of hire and so forth.

In addition to the machine itself you may need to buy some consumables. In the case of a floor sander this will mean the sanding sheets. Often the shop will give you a selection of these and only charge you for those you actually use when you return the machine. The store

ABOVE RIGHT *You may need to hire a good quality grinder to sharpen tools in your existing tool kit.*

RIGHT *A heavy steel roller is a vital tool for ensuring full adhesion of vinyl flooring, but for just this one job it is best to hire.*

BELOW *An electric floor sander will make light work of an otherwise daunting task. Large, edging and corner versions are available.*

should stock and offer you all the necessary safety gear, such as goggles, kneepads and ear defenders, although it is likely you will be obliged to purchase these.

Finding the nearest tool hire store ought to be as simple as looking in the yellow pages or your local phone book. Most reputable firms belong to the HSA (Hire Shops Association) whose address can be found at the back of this book (see page 143). If you have difficulty finding an outlet, phone the HSA and they will be able to tell you the location of your nearest member store.

safety considerations

When undertaking any projects around the home safety should be the number one consideration. There is an element of risk to almost any job and it is vital to minimize such risks by taking all necessary precautions. For example, safety equipment should be considered a vital element of your general tool kit and you will also need to maintain a top quality first aid kit. Above all, never carry out any task that common sense indicates will be dangerous.

ladder safety

Ladders and steps are invaluable for gaining access to higher levels. Although simple tools they are often abused and can lead to nasty accidents if used incorrectly. By obeying the following rules you will minimize the risk of injury.

• The distance from the base of the wall or skirting board to the foot of the ladder must be a quarter of the height the ladder rests at.
• The base of the ladder must rest on a level, non-slip surface.
• Both foot pads must touch the ground   you may shim with plywood pads but keep the ladder level.
• Ensure that the top of the ladder has total contact with the wall surface.

• Before mounting a ladder, check all rungs are secure and have not been damaged in any way.
• If using a ladder outdoors watch out for overhead powerlines and telephone cables.
• Never overstretch   if you cannot reach comfortably, move the ladder.
• When working at any height have a helper hold the bottom of the ladder to prevent it moving.

safety advice

The over-enthusiasm of children and curious nature of animals can lead to accidents. Try to keep these elements clear of the working area!

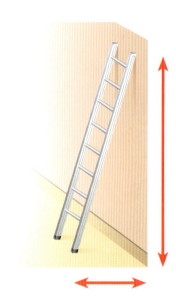

Careful ladder positioning is vital for the safety of its user.

safety equipment

A range of safety equipment is available for various DIY tasks. Some items are intended for particular jobs, but many, such as goggles, work boots and protective gloves, should be worn in most situations. It is also essential to have a well stocked first aid kit to deal with grazes and abrasions.

protective gloves

work boots

lead test kit

plastic gloves

hard hat

ear defenders

goggles

dust mask

respirator mask

knee pads

first aid kit

lifting

Get help when lifting boards and joists. Do not lift more than you can safely carry and when lifting bend your knees, not just your waist. Wear gloves to protect your hands from rough concrete and timber splinters.

dust

Dust can be deadly so always wear a dust mask, which in Europe should be CE marked. Some of the cheaper masks offer little or no protection against certain dusts. Cut tiles and sheet timber outside if possible, particularly when using power tools.

drilling

Never drill into an area of a wall, floor or ceiling where there are likely to be electric cables or gas and water pipes behind. Use a joist, pipe and cable detector to locate the exact position of such services before starting work.

fire risk

Some of the procedures described in this book utilize heat-producing tools, most notably for the removal of paint. Always have a bucket of water or fire extinguisher close at hand when working with such tools, as a small fire can quickly turn into a big fire if it is not quickly put out.

electric cut off

If using electrically operated power tools, it is a good idea to invest in a special cut off device. In the event of the cable being accidentally cut, the device will shut down the electricity supply to the tool. This is commonly called a residual current circuit device or RCD for short.

toxic materials

Some older properties may contain asbestos products or insulation. If you come across suspected asbestos get it removed by a specialist contractor.

Lead was added to paint until fairly recently and can be released into the atmosphere if an old finish is burnt off. Remove lead-based paints with paint stripper before recoating, rather than with a blow-lamp or hot air gun. Modern paints and varnishes are far less toxic but it is still important to follow the instructions on the can, particularly concerning brush cleaning and disposal of excess paint. Remove paint from skin with a proprietary hand cleaner not white spirit, which strips essential oils from the skin and can lead to dermatitis in extreme cases.

Avoid breathing the heavy vapour from adhesives and work in a well ventilated space whenever possible. If you start to feel light headed, stop work immediately and go outside into the fresh air.

TOOL SAFETY

● Before using any unfamiliar tools read and fully understand the manufacturer's instructions. Tools from hire shops should come with an instruction booklet but if you are in any doubt ask for a demonstration before you leave with the tool.

● Chisels, planes and cutting equipment must always be kept as sharp as possible. More accidents are caused by blunt tools slipping on the surface than by sharp tools. An oilstone is ideal to keep tools such as chisels razor sharp.

● Power tools require additional precautions. Unplug any tool before changing bits or blades and never operate with safety guards removed. Regularly inspect cables and wires to ensure they are in good condition. If frayed or damaged they should be replaced to prevent the risk of potentially lethal electric shocks. Although just about every power tool is double insulated for safety, never let a cable trail in water or use a power tool outside in the rain. Power tools in general may also require periodic servicing and accessories, such as bits and blades, should be renewed when necessary, as old ones can strain the workings of the tool.

● Hammers can often slip off nail heads when you are knocking them in. To prevent this, sand the striking face of the hammer to clean it and provide a fine key. This technique may be applied to all types of hammer and is useful for any hammering job.

building materials

In addition to the fixings and adhesives described on pages 34–5, you will require a number of building materials for mixing concrete, fixing floorboards and flooring material, for damp-proofing and for laying insulation material. All the items shown here will be stocked by DIY stores, builder's merchants and flooring outlets, so shop around to see what is available and compare costs.

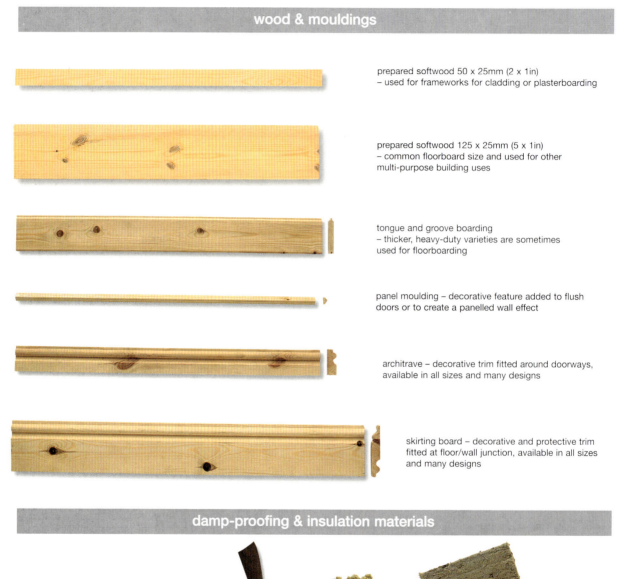

wood & mouldings

prepared softwood 50 x 25mm (2 x 1in)
– used for frameworks for cladding or plasterboarding

prepared softwood 125 x 25mm (5 x 1in)
– common floorboard size and used for other multi-purpose building uses

tongue and groove boarding
– thicker, heavy-duty varieties are sometimes used for floorboarding

panel moulding – decorative feature added to flush doors or to create a panelled wall effect

architrave – decorative trim fitted around doorways, available in all sizes and many designs

skirting board – decorative and protective trim fitted at floor/wall junction, available in all sizes and many designs

damp-proofing & insulation materials

damp-proof membrane (DPM) – laid between subfloor and flooring material to prevent moisture from rising up through concrete and screeds

damp-proof course (DPC) – impermeable membrane sandwiched between layers of masonry in exterior walls, positioned between soil and first floor level, to prevent damp penetrating to interior of house

loose fill insulation – alternative to the mineral wool option

soundproofing insulation slab – used in walls, ceilings and floors

mineral wool – comes in roll or blanket, used for thermal insulation in lofts

timber floorboards – traditional flooring material, can be square-edged (top) or tongue and groove (bottom)

medium-density fibreboard (MDF) – comes in standard (top) or moisture-resistant varieties (bottom), used as a general-purpose building board, manufactured in various thicknesses and sizes

chipboard – generally 18mm ($^{11}/_{16}$in) thick, available in large sheets and square-edged (bottom) or tongue and groove (top) varieties, latter used for flooring

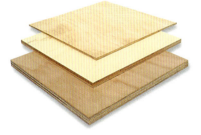

plywood – all-purpose building board made from compressed wooden veneers, available in different thicknesses

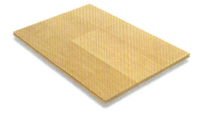

laminate board – chipboard or MDF board usually 9mm ($^{3}/_{8}$in) thick to which is bonded a wood veneer for use as a floor covering

quarry tiles – terracotta-style tile used in kitchens and conservatories, comes in glazed and unglazed varieties

ceramic tiles – floor tiles made of hardened clay, available glazed or unglazed

vinyl tiles – available in self-adhesive or plain for use with an adhesive, wide range of styles and colours

carpet and underlay – normally 3.75m (12ft) wide, with foam or woven backing

builder's sand – added to cement and water to form mortar for building purposes

sharp sand – mixed with cement and water to make screeds and renders

cement – mixed with sand, gravel and water to make mortars and concrete

gravel – mixed with water, sand and cement to form concrete

estimating quantities

Once you have decided that you are going to go ahead with a home improvement project, one of the most important things you will need to work out is the overall cost of the project, so that you can plan your budget and assess whether it is financially viable, then place orders for materials. To do this you will need to make accurate estimates of the quantities required of each component.

planning quantities

In the rush to get started on a new project it is all too easy to miss out sensible planning. Carefully estimating the amount of materials that will be needed is a vital element of the planning stage, so that you can then place an accurate order – standing in the builder's merchant or DIY store is not the time to be working this out. With expensive items, such as quarry tiles and carpet, it is especially important not to over-order or you will be left with costly surplus. Some projects are easier than others when it comes to working out the amount of materials you will need. In the case of a floor in a perfectly square or rectangular room, for instance, simply multiply the width by the length to get the total area. Working in three dimensions is only slightly more complicated – just remember to multiply width by length by depth. The best way to plan for quantities is to take accurate measurements and transfer these to a scale plan, from which you can calculate the amounts.

tips of the trade

Always add about 10% to the final figure when calculating quantities – this will account for cutting and waste and will leave you with a little spare material for future repairs.

SPECIAL CONSIDERATIONS

• **Patterned flooring** – Plan for greater wastage allowance if laying patterned flooring, so that you can match up the design as it is laid.

• **Fitted furniture** – If laying the floor covering in a room with fitted furniture, for example in a kitchen or bathroom, you can cover the entire floor prior to installation, or cut around the furniture leaving a short margin that will run underneath. If the latter, then either incorporate the fitted elements into your plan, if you have an accurate idea of their dimensions, or measure up after installation.

MAKING CALCULATIONS

Depth of joists

The capacity for a joist to support weight is more dependent on depth than thickness, which tends to remain constant at about 50mm (2in). Follow the formula shown below to work out the depth of joist you will need. The number of joists that you require will depend on the size of the room and the centre-to-centre spacing

Formula for calculating depth of joists:

$$\text{Depth in units of 25mm (1in)} = \frac{\text{Span of joists in units of 300mm (1ft)} + 2}{2}$$

Example for room span of 3m (10ft):

$$\text{3m (10ft) divided by 300mm (1ft)} = \frac{10 \text{ units}}{2} = 5 + 2 = 7 \text{ units}$$

7 units x 25mm (1in) = 175mm (7in)

Floor covering

To calculate the amount of floor covering that you need, multiply the width by the length then add 10% for cutting and waste.

Example for a room measuring 3m x 7m (10ft x 23ft):   3 x 5m = 15sq m + 1.5 = 16.5sq m

(10ft x 23ft = 230sq ft + 23 = 253sq ft)

In order to make an accurate calculation of the amount of flooring material needed, it is a good idea to formulate a detailed two-dimensional diagram of the room with measurements for each of the different areas indicated. Even professional builders will make a scale drawing of the room showing the location of principal features. If the room includes permanently fitted furniture, or will do so, these should be included on the diagram, especially if it is not your intention to lay floor covering underneath. Using graph paper to draw the plan will help ensure accuracy. If you take the plan along when going to buy materials, with all the measurements marked on, this will enable you to place an accurate order so that you do not end up with too little or excess surplus.

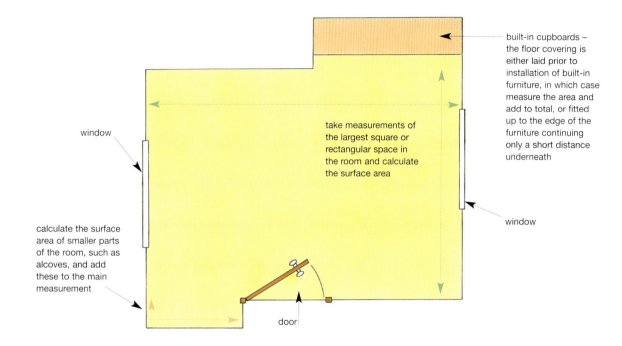

window

calculate the surface area of smaller parts of the room, such as alcoves, and add these to the main measurement

take measurements of the largest square or rectangular space in the room and calculate the surface area

door

built-in cupboards – the floor covering is either laid prior to installation of built-in furniture, in which case measure the area and add to total, or fitted up to the edge of the furniture continuing only a short distance underneath

window

calculating floor covering for stairs

To work out the amount of floor covering needed for a staircase, add together the total run (the sum of the depth of each step) to the total rise (the sum of the height of each step). The total run and total rise can be calculated either by measuring the total width and height of the staircase or by taking measurements for one step and multiplying this by the total number of steps. This will give the 'length' of material required but you will need to mulitply this by the width of the steps to give the total surface area. If laying a trim, whereby strips of the staircase are left exposed either side of the covering, adjust the width measurement accordingly. Add 5% to the total for cutting and waste.

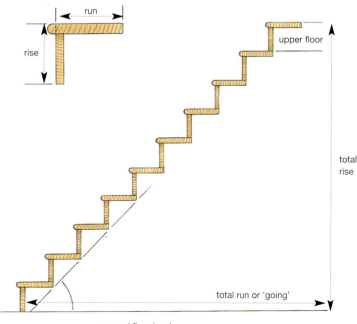

run

rise

upper floor

total rise

total run or 'going'

ground floor level

making changes to floors

Making changes to existing flooring, or replacing the floor altogether, is often the first step towards more general renovation of a room. For example, if you are converting an upper-storey room into a bathroom you will need to consider strengthening joists to cope with the weight of a bath filled to capacity. You may be forced to make changes due to adverse circumstances, such as damp penetration in a suspended floor, the best remedy for which is often to replace it altogether with a solid concrete floor. Prevention is the best cure, however, and another project described in this chapter is how to add ventilation to the underfloor area in order to avoid damage from damp.

41

By installing a plywood floor over the concrete subfloor, this garage has been transformed into a comfortable workroom.

laying floors in bathrooms

If you feel confident about laying floors in any other room in the house then the bathroom should present no particular problem. However, there are a few special considerations, most of which relate to all the water involved in the day-to-day activities that take place – bathrooms can be extremely wet and measures need to be taken to minimize the amount of moisture damage to the floor. The damp air, leaking pipes from baths and basins and the weight of the tub all conspire to cause damage to both the subfloor and floor covering.

dealing with moisture

To ensure the longevity of flooring in a bathroom, an adequate ventilation system is essential to eradicate the presence of condensation. Care over plumbing work and regular inspections will make sure that all pipework connections are tight and leak free. Laying bath mats will go some way to minimize the damage due to splashes from baths and basins, but more important is to ensure the floor covering is waterproof or resistant to moisture and that all areas where moisture can penetrate are adequately sealed. Before laying any new floor covering carefully inspect the existing subfloor for water damage and rot. Remove the bath panel and check below the bathtub. Leaking pipes should be obvious and need to be rectified immediately. A musty smell is a sure sign of problems and must not be ignored, sections of the floor that are soft or rotten will need to be replaced. If you are buying sheets of manufactured board, remember to tell your supplier that these are being laid in a bathroom, as there are special water resistant grades which are better suited to the damp environment.

ABOVE RIGHT *Naturally water resistant, hard tiles are a good option for bathrooms, but make sure you seal the grout joints.*

the bathroom suite

If the flooring is being replaced or re-laid as part of an overall bathroom refurbishment the suite is probably also being replaced at the same time. If not, then before the floor can be replaced you will need to remove the bathroom suite and any other cabinets and fixtures attached to the floor. Elsewhere in this book you will find instructions on renewing the subfloor and provided you follow these closely you should encounter few problems. When flooring is to be replaced as part of a much larger refurbishment program it can be a good idea to lay the floor covering before the installation of toilet, bath, bidet and basin pedestal. Though not always practical, where it is you avoid having to lay the floor covering in what is often a tight space that will require lots of fiddly cutting.

LEFT *A neater job will often result if floor coverings can be laid before the installation of the bathroom suite.*

By using whole sheets the lack of cutting means you are able to put down the floor much faster and will end up with a neater finish. Moreover, because the suite sits on top of the flooring there will be less chance of water finding its way onto the subfloor. The only drawback is that you need to be careful not to damage the floor during the installation of the suite and when the plumbing and decoration is carried out, but even then the floor may be protected with just a few sheets of hardboard.

weight considerations

If you are installing a larger bath you will need to take into account the stresses this may impose on the floor. Replacing a standard bath with a jacuzzi will add about an extra 225kg (500lb) when the bath is full. It is quite likely that you will need to add some local strengthening to the joist, and the floorboards may be too thin to support the weight of the feet. If you are at all concerned then you should consult a structural engineer, who will be able to assess the risks and recommend a course of action. You will have to pay for this of course but it is better than having the bath end up in the downstairs living room!

ABOVE RIGHT *A bathroom looks far neater when pipework is concealed behind wall panels and under floorboards.*

MIDDLE RIGHT *A bath holds a considerable amount of water, which puts an enormous load on the floor and may mean you need to add extra strengthening around large bathtubs.*

BELOW *If you are leaving exposed timber floorboards in a bathroom you will need to apply a water-resistant finish.*

types of flooring

Almost any type of flooring can be used in a bathroom – even hardwood floors can be treated with a water-resistant finish. Check with your supplier whether the flooring you intend to buy is suitable for bathrooms. Carpet is best avoided as water can soak through and rot both the carpet and the subfloor underneath, although there are varieties of carpet specifically designed for bathrooms which are water, mildew and stain resistant with a backing that does not allow water to seep into the pad. Tile and sheet vinyl floors are probably the best choices as they are easy to clean and effectively resist staining and moisture penetration. Whatever flooring you choose, always use waterproof adhesives and grout, and seal holes with silicone where pipes come through the floor. Moisture resistant flooring and MDF have a green tinge to them, so can be easily identified against standard products which are usually biscuit colour.

laying floors for garages & workrooms

Most garage floors are made from concrete, which is fine for the car but can be hard on feet and legs. Moreover, a concrete floor tends to be cold and damp and if you are storing tools or machinery this is liable to cause them to rust. A plywood floor will make for a drier, more comfortable room.

making changes

44

Garages are often used for hobby rooms and children's play areas, but without some modification they can be cold and uninviting. By adding a floating floor the garage can be transformed into a comfortable activity area. Plywood floors are easier on the knees and allow for a floor covering. They are simple to lay and since they are not fixed to the subfloor, they can be removed at a later date.

tools for the job

club hammer & bolster chisel
mixing equipment
broom
tape measure & pencil
trimming knife
handsaw
cordless drill/driver

1 Use a club hammer and bolster chisel to knock off any high points on the concrete that could puncture the plastic membrane. Fill any large indentations with a concrete or mortar mix. Sweep the floor to remove any dust and debris.

2 Lay down the damp-proof membrane (DPM), allowing it to lip up the wall by at least 150mm (6in). Trim off any excess with a trimming knife. If you need to attach two sheets together, tape along the join with duct tape, then fold the second sheet over on itself three or four times so that you end up with a seam 100mm (4in) wide, before taping again.

3 Starting at one wall, place 100 x 50mm (4 x 2in) timbers side down on top of the DPM at 600mm (2ft) intervals. Use a handsaw to cut them to length. Then cut some noggins to provide support at the end joints and between timbers, attached at 1.2m (3ft 11in) intervals.

4 Cut some polystyrene insulation panels to fit between the timbers and lay them in position. 50mm (2in) thick panels will sit level with the top of the timbers and provide additional support for the flooring. You can omit the insulation if you wish, but it does make a big difference to the warmth of the room and provides some measure of sound insulation.

5 Take 18mm ($^{11}/_{16}$in) shuttering plywood and, with its best side uppermost, drill pilot holes at 200mm (8in) intervals, 50mm (2in) in from the edge and across the centre of the board. Screw down the boards using 32mm ($1^5/_{16}$in) no 8 screws. Unless the room is perfectly square, you may find that you have to trim the edges of some of the boards.

safety advice

When cutting the heavy plywood sheets, make sure they are well supported on a sawhorse, workmate or trestles. You will be able to cut more accurately and the sheets are much less likely to slip and cause an injury.

6 Moulding or skirting boards provide a neat trim and help to hold down the edges of the floor. Screw through the skirting boards and damp-proof membrane into the wall. Fold but do not cut the plastic at the corners of the room, tucking it neatly behind the skirting as you fix it back.

7 Run a sharp trimming knife around the top of the skirting to trim off any excess plastic flush. If you do not like the look of the DPM sandwiched between the skirting board and the wall, this can be disguised by running a bead of mastic along the top of the skirting.

8 At door openings, fit threshold cover strips to hide the edges of the plywood. If the new floor is higher than the floor level in an the adjoining room, then you will need to make a ramped reducer strip and cut the bottom of the door to suit. With garage up-and-over doors, screw or nail a thin strip of timber to cover the joint between timber and ply. Ensure the plastic is sandwiched in-between, then trim the plastic level with the finished floor.

FLOOR COVERINGS

If the room is to be used for a children's play area you could cover the plywood with stick down tiles or vinyl sheeting. For a deluxe finish a piece of carpet will offer a measure of thermal and noise insulation.

👍
tips of the trade

Cutting polystyrene can be messy as the white lumps stick to everything. Rather than use a saw, which generates large amounts of static, a sharp, serrated bread knife is almost as fast and a good deal cleaner.

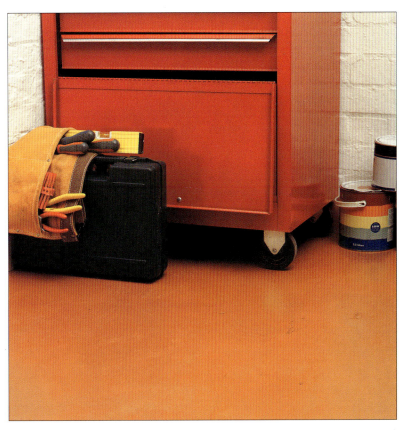

Sturdy and damp-proof, a plywood floor is ideal for transforming a garage into a workshop, and a further covering of vinyl will add extra warmth and comfort.

replacing a suspended floor with concrete ⁄⁄⁄⁄

There may be several reasons for replacing a suspended floor with concrete. One of the most likely scenarios is when the original floor has suffered from rot or infestation and will have to be replaced. In older houses unprotected by a damp-proof course a concrete floor might be installed as part of the overall damp-proofing measures in the property.

tools for the job

tape measure & pencil
spirit level
prybar
hand saw
bolster & chisel
shovel
punner
scissors
small cement mixer
tamping board
plasterer's trowels

1 Before stripping out the old flooring, make a pencil mark 1m (3ft) up the wall. Draw a line around the room at this height with a spirit level – this is your datum mark.

2 Strip out the old floorboards and joists. Joists are easier to handle cut into sections, especially on older floors where they will need to be pulled out of wall sockets. Ensure all traces of the old joists have been removed, this is especially important if dry rot has been present.

3 Shovel in a layer of hardcore so that its top level is 1.3m (4ft 3in) below the level of the datum mark on the wall. Use a punner to tamp it down and break up any large lumps.

4 The next stage is to lay on the sand blinding. Shovel builder's sand on top of the hardcore to a depth of 100mm (4in), all the time checking the height against the datum marks on the wall. You may find it helpful to cut a batten to 1.2m (3ft 11in) rather than keep measuring with the tape measure. Smooth it down with the back of your shovel as you go and use a long board to make certain that the sand is flat.

5 Lay a sheet of plastic damp-proof membrane on top of the sand, taking care not to puncture the sheet. Ensure that it lips up the wall by about 300mm (1ft). Use some strips of duct tape to hold the membrane against the wall.

6 Reinforcing bars strengthen the concrete and prevent it from cracking. Place the bars raised up on concrete garden slabs. Make a criss-cross pattern, at 400mm (1ft 4in) centres, tying any joints with binding wire. Keep the bars at least 100mm (4in) clear of any wall. Once finished, the grid should be fairly rigid and should not sag if you walk on it.

7 Provided another person helps, for a small room it is perfectly feasible to mix the concrete yourself with a small mixer. Use a mix of 1 part ordinary Portland cement, 1 part building sand and 3 parts aggregate. There is no need to be too precise, just measure each of the components out by the shovel-full. Do not make the concrete overly wet – add just enough water to mix the components into a grey creamy consistency.

8 Rather than simply spreading the concrete in a random fashion, start in one corner of the room and work back towards the doorway. Use the shovel to work the concrete down between the reinforcing bars, forcing out any trapped air.

9 Check the top level of the concrete against the datum with a batten cut to 1m (3ft), to ensure the finished floor will not be lower than adjacent rooms.

10 Tamp the concrete surface with a board or piece of 18mm (¹¹⁄₁₆in) thick ply. Starting at one end of the room, work the top of the concrete with the tamp edge. Do not apply great force but simply stipple the surface slightly. If the room is over 2.5m (8ft) wide you will need a helper. If you work towards the doorway tamping as you go, the holes left by your boots will refill.

11 After a couple of hours water will have come to the surface before it starts to sink back into the concrete. At this point you can trowel the surface to a smooth finish with metal plasterer's trowels. Spread your weight on two ply boards about 800mm (2ft 7in) square. Gently lift the leading edge of the trowel to stop it digging in as you drag it across. Work back towards the doorway, moving the boards as you go.

12 You can walk on the concrete the next day, but leave at least three days before trimming off the plastic and fitting skirting. Wait at least three weeks if laying carpet as moisture remaining in the concrete will rot the backing.

installing joist hangers

On most modern houses the ends of the joists are supported on metal brackets called joist hangers. Even if you are replacing the entire floor in an older house where joist hangers were not originally fitted, you can still fit them using the method described below. There are several different types of hangers and each type comes in different sizes, so make sure you fit the correct joist hangers for your application.

The most common reason for installing joist hangers is when a new floor is being built, either for a new room or because the original joists need replacing. Joist hangers are typically fixed to either masonry or timberwork. In new houses the joist hangers are built into the wall, or if the house is timber-framed special hangers are nailed to the studwork. In older house where joists are fitted into pockets in the wall, by installing joist hangers the ends are kept away from potentially damp brickwork and masonry. Joist hangers also allow you to space the joists so that the joints of sheet flooring fall directly onto the centreline of a joist.

tools for the job

tape measure & pencil

spirit level

cordless drill/driver

panel saw

hammer

trimming knife

1 Allow for the width of the plasterboard by measuring up 12mm ($^9/_{16}$in) from where the underside of the ceiling will be, then mark a level line at this point all around the room using a spirit level. Mark out the centre spacing for the joists along this line no more than 400mm (1ft 4in) apart centre to centre. You may need additional joists close to the wall in order to support the edge of the boards.

tips of the trade

• **Positioning joists** – Joists typically run across the shortest span of the room, but loadbearing walls must always support the ends. If you are replacing a floor the new joists should run the same way as the original joists. Consult an architect or structural engineer for advice if you are unsure.

• **Spacing joists** – The spacing of floor joists is always quoted as centre to centre. This is the spacing between the imaginary centreline of each joist. To gain the actual distance between joists, deduct the total thickness of one complete joist.

2 To ensure the finished floor ends up level, nail or screw a temporary batten to the wall so that the top edge is level with your datum mark. Hold the joist hangers on top of the batten at the centreline reference marks and screw or nail them to the wall. If using screws you may find it easier to mark the screw position before drilling the hole and inserting a wall plug. Use a hammer or percussion drill fitted with a bit specifically designed for masonry when drilling into brick or blockwork.

If the hole has been drilled correctly you should be able simply to push in the wall plug for a snug fit.

3 Get a helper to hold the end of the tape measure while you check the length of the joists. Measure by holding the tape across the room and checking the distance between the back plates of the joist hangers. As it is unlikely that the room will be completely square, hence lengths will vary slightly, do not just measure the first joist and assume all the others will be the same length. Deduct 4mm ($^3/_{16}$in) from the overall measurement and mark this on the joist before cutting to length with a panel saw.

4 If you have cut it correctly the joist should drop in without the need for hitting it with a hammer. If the joist wobbles from side to side slightly in the hanger, you can make it a better fit by wrapping roofing felt around the end and securing it in place with nails. Parcelling the end in felt also has the added advantage of preventing moisture from wicking into the end grain of the joist.

5 Nail the joists into position through a couple of the holes on either side of the hangers. Galvanized nails have a better grip due to their rough finish and are more resistant to rust than conventional brightwire nails. Nails should be no more than half the thickness of the joist or there is a risk of splitting the timber. Do not drive them right home at this stage. Place the spirit level across all the joists and check for level, repeating this at several places in the room. If any joists are high, pull the nails and either trim a little from the underside of the joist where it sits in the hanger or reposition the hanger. When you are certain of the fit, drive home the temporary nails and hammer nails through the

remaining holes in the sides of the joist hangers. To avoid splitting the wood try blunting the ends of the nails with light hammer blows.

6 For any span more than 3m (10ft), nail herringbone struts between each of the joists to add extra strength and to prevent twisting (see pages 122–3). The joists are now ready to receive the flooring and ceiling, but before doing this run in any cables and plumbing work (see pages 50–1).

LATERAL RESTRAINT STRAPS

For extra stability to the completed floor you may want to add lateral restraint straps. These come in the form of galvanized steel straps, fitted and screwed to the wall, and are available from any good builder's merchant. Such restraint straps are intended to be fitted at a perpendicular angle to the joists.

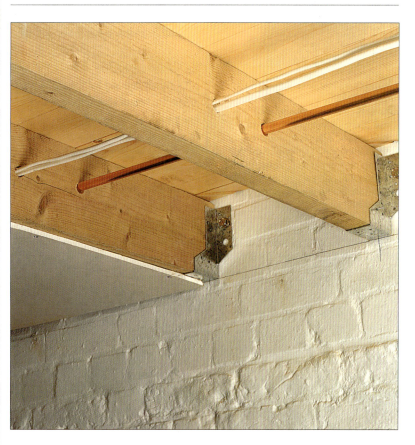

Provided they are fitted with care and accuracy, joist hangers will form a sturdy suspended floor with the added benefit of a damp-proof barrier.

cutting an access hatch ⁄⁄⁄⁄

There can be lots of reasons for wanting to gain access to the area underneath a floor, but the most common is for the repair or installation of services such as plumbing or wiring. Before the introduction of chipboard and ply floors, accessing was usually a simple matter of lifting and replacing a few boards. Sheet materials, which cover larger expanses, make access a more complicated affair, since removing sections is not really an option and small access hatches need to be cut into the floor instead.

Using the speed and versatility of an electric router, cutting an access hatch in a chipboard, ply or laminate floor need not be complicated. The techniques demonstrated here allow access to be gained with a minimal amount of disruption to the overall floor. Cutting permanent hatches also means that the area under the floor can be easily accessed whenever the need arises in the future.

chipboard & ply floors

tools for the job

tape measure & pencil
screwdriver
electric router & 'rout-a-bout' jig

1 A 'rout-a-bout' is a type of jig specially made for use with an electric router. It is fast and easy to use for those with some previous experience with routers. First mark the position of the access hatch on the floor. Attach the electric router to

the special base plate, then loosely screw the plate to the floor, directly over the area you wish to cut. Rotate the router around the screw until the disc is cut all the way round.

2 Remove the disc and drop in a special plastic ring, which will come supplied with the 'rout-a-bout'.

3 Finally, drop the cut disc so that it rests on the plastic ring. No glue or fixing of any kind is required and the area surrounding the hatch is almost as strong as the floor prior to the hole being cut. Access to the underfloor area is available at any time by simply lifting out the disc.

laminate floors

When a laminate or solid timber floor has been laid over a ply or chipboard subfloor, it is vital to be as neat as possible. The cut out section can be any size, but making it as small as is practicable will mean it is ultimately less obtrusive.

tools for the job

safety equipment
tape measure & pencil
carpenter's square
fine-toothed panel saw
double-sided tape
router
wood chisel
handsaw

1 Mark out a square on the floor 300mm (1ft) along each side. Check each corner is a perfect right angle with a carpenter's square. Two of the sides must also be parallel with the line of the laminate strips.

2 Prepare some battens 60mm (2½in) wide and no less than 10mm (½in) thick. Stick the battens to the floor with double-sided tape, ensuring that the inside edges exactly align with the pencil marks.

3 Insert a 10mm (½in) thick straight cutter into the router and attach the template guide bush to the base plate. Keeping the base plate down on the battens with the bush against the inside of the battens, cut through the laminate floor and the subfloor.

safety advice

Using a router is noisy and dusty so wear always a dust mask, goggles and ear defenders.

tips of the trade

Make sure that the router cutters are sharp to avoid splintering the top surface of the laminate.

4 Remove the section of floor and put to one side. Carefully peel off the battens and double-sided tape. Change the router cutter to a bearing-guided cutter and run a rebate around the inside of the opening, cutting down to the same depth as the thickness of the laminate.

5 Use a sharp wood chisel to square up the rounded internal corners of the laminate left by the circular router cutter.

6 Form a section of flooring from some laminate offcuts that is at least 2.5cm (1in) larger all round than

the hole in the floor. Glue the tongues together with wood glue, then glue this in turn onto the section of chipboard or ply subfloor that you saved. Put a heavy weight on top and allow the glue to dry.

7 Make a paper or card template so that it just drops into the rebated opening in the floor, then clearly mark the positions of the joint lines onto the top edges. Transfer the template to the replacement floor section, noting the position of the joints but keeping it as near the centre as possible. Mark around the outside before finally cutting with a fine-toothed panel saw. Sand up the edges to remove any rough spots.

8 Provided that the cutting and marking have been accurate, the panel should simply drop into position and require no further fixing. If you are confident that you will never need access later, it could be glued in place. If the panel is quite large you may want to use small brass screws at each corner to retain it.

soundproofing a floor

Noise pollution can be a cause of friction between neighbours, especially in apartment blocks and properties where floors have been divided into separate flats, though the problem can be just as bad within families. Adding some soundproofing to a floor helps to cut down noise transmitted from above and will go some way to solving your noise pollution problem. Using the technique shown here almost any floor can be soundproofed.

Noise is either transmitted through the air or through the materials used in the construction of a house. With the method of soundproofing shown here, sand and insulation blanket combine to form an effective barrier against the transmission of noise throughout the house. A floor can be soundproofed from below, but this means destroying the ceiling, and working above your head is tiring on the arms and neck. Moreover, by soundproofing from above, sand can be used as an insulating material, which is both a cheap and effective sound-deadening medium.

safety advice

The soundproofing method shown here will increase the weight of the floor. Before starting any work you must check that this will not adversely effect the structural integrity of the property. If you are in any doubt then contact a structural engineer.

tools for the job

pipe, cable & joist detector
crayon
circular saw
trimming knife
gloves
prybar
bolster chisel
hammer
handsaw
cordless drill/driver
dust mask

1 Unless they are immediately obvious, use a pipe and wiring detector to check the position of plumbing and electrical circuits. Then mark their positions on the floor surface with a crayon, so that when cutting into the floor you will be able avoid damaging these services.

2 If the floor is constructed of chipboard or tongue and groove boards, run a circular saw set to the thickness of the flooring down the joints between boards. Do not cut round more than one or two boards at this stage, for once you start lifting the first couple of boards you may find that the rest can be removed without cutting off the tongues.

3 Use a prybar and bolster to gently lift the flooring, trying not to damage too many boards. Remove any nails that remain poking out of the joists with the claw end of a hammer.

tips of the trade

With all the floorboards removed it can be difficult to move around the room. Have a couple of loose boards to hand that you can position across the joists to walk on as you work in the room.

4 Screw 50 x 25mm (2 x 1in) battens to either side of the ceiling joists. Make sure the bottom edge is just clear of the ceiling below.

5 Cut 12mm (⁹⁄₁₆in) plywood strips to sit on top of the battens. Fix the strips in place with nails.

6 Cut plastic membrane material to line the troughs, pressing it into the corners and allowing it to lip up the sides of the joists. Nail or staple it into position using a minimum of fastenings near the top edge. Trim off excess plastic membrane so that it is level with the top of the joists.

7 Pour in kiln dried sand to about 50mm (2in) deep. Cut a piece of ply so it rests on top of the joists with the bottom edge 50mm (2in) higher

than the bottom of the trough. Use this to to achieve consistent results when levelling out the sand.

8 Place slabs of rock wool on top of the sand. They should not be any higher than the top of the joists or refixing the boards will be difficult. If cutting the slabs, use a fine handsaw and make sure you wear a dust mask.

9 With the two layers of insulating material in place, you can refit the flooring on top of the joists. Any split or damaged boards will need to be replaced. When refixing boards make sure that all joints are tight and there are no gaps. Covering the floor with some thick, good quality underlay and carpet will further enhance the soundproofing properties.

If appropriate to the type of floor covering, a thick underlay stapled to the subfloor will further enhance the sound insulation properties of the floor.

adding ventilation to floors ⚒⚒⚒

Ventilation is essential in any floor space. Stagnant air can lead to rot, unpleasant smells and damp, which can destroy floor finishes and carpets, and in some cases the floor itself, if left untreated. Some floors suffer from a lack of ventilation more than others, such as those in bathrooms and kitchens. Before starting on major work it is worth checking that poor ventilation is not simply a case of existing air bricks being blocked by soil and dirt.

fitting a floor grille

Though not as effective as an exterior air brick, a grille fitted into floorboards will allow air to circulate in the floor space, which might otherwise be a potential breeding ground for rot and infestation. If the grille is installed under a window or a radiator then the convection currents will help to draw air into the room.

tools for the job

joist detector

tape measure & pencil

cordless drill/driver

jigsaw or padsaw

bradawl or small drill

screwdriver

1 Determine the positions of the joists. These are often indicated by the position of the floor fixings or you can use a joist detector. Measure in and draw a parallel line 150mm (6in) out from the skirting board. Place the top edge of the grille on this line and draw a pencil line round it, keeping

the ends equally spaced between the run of joists where these run at right angles to the wall.

🖐 safety advice

When determining the position of the grille, use a detector to locate pipes and cables to avoid cutting through these services by accident.

2 Set the grille to one side and draw another line 12mm (⁹⁄₁₆in) inside the grille outline. Drill a hole at each corner with a 12mm (⁹⁄₁₆in) drill bit, ensuring that the edges of the bit stay inside the second guideline.

3 Cut out the waste area within the second guideline, using either a jigsaw or padsaw. Work from each drilled hole. At the last hole the waste section is liable to fall through into the ceiling area. To prevent this, particularly if the grille is so small that you will not be able to get your hand into the hole to remove the cut out section, partially screw in a large wood screw to give you something to hold as the block is cut away.

👍 tips of the trade

When a grille is to be fitted into a polished floor you will want to get the best finish possible. Special jigsaw blades are available that cut on the down stroke and prevent splintering to the floor surface.

4 Remove any rough edges from the hole with abrasive paper before screwing on the grille. Align the edges of the grille with the pencil guideline. Use a bradawl or small drill to make a pilot hole for the screws and fix the grille in position. For a neater appearance, align all the screw slots so that they face the same way.

5 Where carpet is to be refitted, cut out the hole in the carpeting prior to fitting the grille in place. Then screw down the grille so that the carpet is sandwiched between grille and floorboards. If the carpet is quite thick pile, you may find that you need to use slightly longer screws than those that were originally supplied with the grille.

fitting an air brick

Exterior air bricks are the traditional means of ventilating the space under suspended floors at ground level. Alterations to the house or garden may mean that the original bricks are no longer performing their function. As a general rule there should be an air brick every 2.5m (8ft) along an external wall. If there are less air bricks in the walls of your house, or if you have signs of mould or damp due to lack of air movement, you should consider fitting additional bricks. Air bricks come in a variety of sizes but the easiest to fit are the smaller ones, used here, which have the same overall dimensions as a common house brick.

tools for the job

cordless drill/driver

club hammer & bolster chisel

protective gloves & goggles

pointing trowel

jointing trowel

1 To install an additional air brick, or replace one that is missing, first select a suitable standard brick to remove, 2–2.5m (6½–8ft) from the nearest existing air brick. It should also be at least one course below the damp-proof course and below the level of the floor inside. Drill lots of holes to break up the brick, using an electric drill with a large masonry bit.

2 Remove the remainder of the brick with a club hammer and bolster chisel, taking great care not to damage the adjacent brickwork. Most of the mortar holding the brick in place will probably come away with the brick. Remove any remaining mortar so that you have a clean hole ready to receive the air brick.

3 Mix up some mortar using 3 parts sand to 1 part cement. Cut a couple of strips of timber 50mm (2in) long with a square section the same thickness as the existing mortar courses in the brick wall. Place the strips in the bottom of the hole and hold them in place with a little mortar. Damp down the new brick and spread mortar onto the top and ends.

4 Slide in the brick, ensuring it stays flush with the existing brickwork. Check with a straightedge that the brick is not too far in or sitting proud. Work in additional mortar to the joint with a pointing trowel, if necessary. After about an hour when the mortar has just started to harden, finish with a jointing trowel.

tips of the trade

When pointing brickwork, leave the mortar to 'go off' a little before finishing. In this way you will not drag mortar out of the join and the finish will be smoother.

floor finishes

There are probably more choices of floor covering available today then there have ever been. Improvements and innovations within manufacturing mean that materials previously deemed unsuitable are now commonly used for flooring. Many homeowners still make carpet their first choice and it is easy to see why – luxurious underfoot, a carpet will lend any room a warm and cosy feel. Other types of floor covering are also finding their way into homes. Laminate flooring, which has always been popular in Scandinavia, is now common in other European countries. Many people still tend to avoid sheet flooring, but this too has had something of a renaissance in recent years, and a huge range is now available that has little in common with the linoleum of old.

Floor finishes need not start and end with carpets – hard tiles, for example, can make a stylish and original flooring option.

comparing floor coverings

When planning out alterations to a room it is essential to know which types of floor covering are appropriate for the particular subfloor, what are the specific qualities of each type and how much it is all likely to cost. The following table examines each of the main types of floor covering available to buy, listing the cost, positive and negative aspects, suitability and how difficult it is to lay, so that you can easily compare types and make your choice.

PROS & CONS	COST	DURABILITY	LAYING	SUITABLE SUBFLOORS
CARPET ▼				
Pros Warm and soft to the touch. Luxurious look. Vast range of colours and patterns to suit any colour scheme. Helps to keep down draughts. Available in wide rolls. **Cons** Not waterproof but special carpets are available for bathrooms. Can mark and stain easily.	Wide range of costs from cheap to very expensive.	Moderately durable. Carpets with a high wool content last longest and can be shampooed.	May be undertaken by a skilled amateur but more expensive carpets are best left to a professional. Cheaper foam-backed carpet is glued to double-sided tape at the edges. Woven backed carpet is attached to gripper rods at the edges of the room.	Concrete screed, plywood, chipboard and solid timber floors are all suitable, but carpet is generally laid on top of underlay.
WOODBLOCK ▼				
Pros Very hardwearing. Easy to maintain. Can be stained or bleached to give different look. **Cons** Limited range of options as not all timbers are suitable for floors.	Expensive but some modern equivalents are slightly cheaper.	Very durable – ideal for high traffic areas. When worn, scuffed and dirty can be refinished to bring back to a condition that is good as new.	Laying proper woodblock flooring is a professional job requiring hot pitch. An experienced amateur using a latex adhesive can lay small areas.	Concrete screed. Not suitable for upper floors or for laying on wooden floorboards.
VINYL TILES ▼				
Pros Hardwearing. Easy to maintain and keep clean. Waterproof when correctly laid. Ideal for kitchens and bathrooms. **Cons** Not suitable for living areas as they can look rather clinical. Cold and hard.	Costs are moderate considering the life span and compared to other coverings.	Very durable – ideal for high traffic areas. Mopping or wiping with a cloth is all that is required in the way of maintenance.	Easy to lay, provided the subfloor is in good condition and the setting out is correct. Self-adhesive tiles are the cleanest and easiest to lay for the amateur. Others are set into adhesive.	Concrete screed. Ply or chipboard. Solid floorboards should be covered with ply or hardboard before laying.

PROS & CONS	COST	DURABILITY	LAYING	SUITABLE SUBFLOORS
SHEET VINYL ▼				
Pros Hardwearing. Easy to maintain. Waterproof when correctly laid – ideal for kitchens and bathrooms. Available in wide rolls. **Cons** Not as resilient as tiles. Not suitable for living areas as it can look uninviting.	Moderate considering the life span and compared to other coverings.	Very durable – ideal for high traffic areas. Mopping or wiping with a cloth is all that is required in the way of maintenance.	Not as easy to lay as tiles as it can be unwieldy. Often best to make a template first. Some can be loose laid but others are glued to the subfloors with special adhesive.	Concrete screed. Ply or chipboard. Solid timber floorboards should be covered with ply or hardboard before laying.
LAMINATE ▼				
Pros Hardwearing. Easy to maintain. Look of solid wood without the expense. Does not need to be laid by a professional. **Cons** Difficult to affect an invisible repair. Can be noisy and slippery. Limited range of finishes.	Moderate considering the life span and in comparison with other coverings. The cheaper laminates are better suited to low-usage rooms.	Durable. Ideal for high traffic areas. Mopping or wiping with a cloth is all that is required in the way or maintenance.	Straightforward to lay. Some of the new versions clip together and do not require glue, making them even easier. All should be laid on a thin underlay which varies according to the type of subfloor.	Concrete screed. Ply or chipboard. Solid timber floorboards should be covered with ply or hardboard before laying.
PLYWOOD ▼				
Pros Hardwearing. Best suited for workrooms and garages. **Cons** Dusty if not coated. Fixings cannot be concealed.	Cheap to moderate depending on the thickness and grade of ply chosen.	Very durable. Ideal for high traffic areas. Waterproof when a suitable paint or varnish is applied.	Simple with no complicated joints but take care fitting around pipes. Nailed or screwed to the subfloor or joists.	Laid directly onto joists or flooring. DPM underneath if laid on floor liable to become damp.
QUARRY TILES ▼				
Pros Hardwearing. Easy to maintain. Waterproof when correctly laid and sealed. Ideal for kitchens and entrances. **Cons** Noisy, hard and cold. Slippery when wet. Crockery dropped onto it will smash.	Highly expensive.	Very durable. Ideal for high traffic areas. Unsealed tiles need periodic sealing with a proprietary product in order to retain their appearance and prevent the surface staining.	Not a suitable job for novice. Tiles are laid in wet mortar rather than an adhesive.	Concrete screed. Ply or chipboard. Solid timber floorboards should be covered with ply or hardboard before laying.

types of floor tiles

The variety of tiles available for flooring has expanded greatly in the past thirty years. It is now possible to choose from numerous styles and designs and from a range of different materials, including vinyl, cork, carpet, ceramic and stone tiles. Provided they are properly laid, floor tiles are functional, sturdy and can last a lifetime.

considering floor tiles

Not so many years ago the variety of tiles available for domestic situations were extremely limited. All this has changed and now there are a plethora of designs and finishes to suit just about every room in the house and to satisfy the decorative taste of almost any homeowner. Advances in tiling adhesives mean tiles that were once only suitable for professional fitting can now be laid by competent DIY enthusiasts. Another thing to bear in mind is that tiles are often easier to handle and transport than sheet materials as they come in small packages that are easier to carry. Even for a moderate sized room, a carpet is heavy and unwieldy and for an inexperienced person can be impossible to lay unaided. Tiles, on the other hand, are far more manageable since they can be collected in the back of the car, taken home and laid without help.

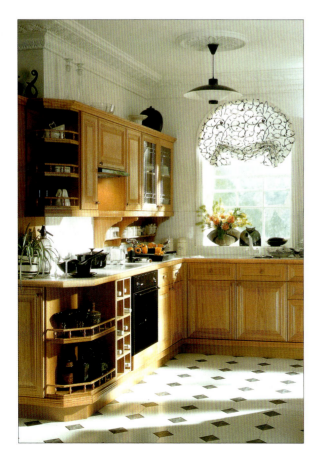

costs

One of the reasons that tiles have become so popular is because the variety of materials and designs are endless, and with this comes a wide range of pricing. The most expensive tiles are the hard tile varieties, such as ceramic, stone and slate. In the past, slate floors were laid in workmen's cottages and cheaper houses, but nowadays these styles have become very desirable. Stone and slate flooring that replicates an antique look is very expensive and the cost of laying is likely to be a small proportion of the final overall cost. Although hard tiles are costly in themselves, the extra expense at the outset is likely to pay off in the long run because hard tiles are extremely durable and likely to last a lifetime. If you want the look of a hard tile design without the expense, vinyl tiles are often designed to imitate the appearance of hard tiles. When planning to

TOP *Cork tiles are comfortable underfoot and easily cleaned, making them a good choice for bathrooms.*

LEFT *These vinyl tiles have been designed to imitate the look of a patterned hard tile floor when fully laid.*

install tile floors, the most important tasks are mapping out what tiles are suitable for specific rooms and preparing a budget for materials and installation. If not planned properly a tiling project can easily go over budget. It is best to shop around to learn about variety and affordability before deciding what tile flooring will work best in your home.

choosing types

Rather than placing all tiles into the same category, it helps to split them up into hard, soft, and semi-rigid types. In the hard category you will find tiles such as ceramic, mosaic and quarry. Quarry tiles look homely and give a kitchen a warm, rustic feel, but many find them hard and unforgiving. Soft tiles include carpet, soft rubber and some cork varieties. Carpet tiles have long been a favourite in office buildings, but are now being manufactured specifically for the domestic market and have can used to good effect in homes. In between these two are the semi-rigid types, such as vinyl tiles. It is best to enquire at your local tile merchant's what is the most appropriate use for the tile variety you select. Not all types of tiles are appropriate for every room in the home. It is crucial to consider the desired function for the tile flooring as well as the foundation on which that floor will be laid. For example, quarry tiles are liable to be too heavy to lay on a suspended floor and the kitchen is probably not the best place for carpet tiles, where they are likely to get very stained. When making your choice of tiles you need not be confined to squares and rectangles – octagonal and hexagonal tiles are available if slightly harder

ABOVE *An impressive fitted appearance has here been achieved by continuing these large mosaic tiles along the walls and around the bath.*

BELOW LEFT *Hard tiles are an increasingly popular option for use as a floor covering in the main living space of a home.*

to lay. When choosing tiles that you intend to lay yourself, be realistic about your skill levels. Laying soft tiles requires little in the way of experience and equipment and a good quality tool kit will usually suffice. Many hard tiling projects, however, are likely to require greater skill and more specialist tools for the jobs of mixing and spreading the mortar, cutting edge tiles and grouting.

choosing styles

If you are considering a floor tiling project in your home, it is important to make a selection that you will be able live with for a long time. Tiling materials and designs must be chosen with an eye to the future. What might be appealing to you today could change as your tastes and family needs alter, and what might seem like a good idea now could be a choice that you live to regret in years to come, especially after you have gone to great expense to install a new tile floor. The colour of the walls or the curtains are likely to change several times during the lifetime of the tiles, so it may be wise to opt for neutral colours. It is best to use bold patterns and colours as accents only. If you desire a more dramatic design, it might be wise to use cheaper tiles that can be more easily changed.

laying chipboard & ply floors

Chipboard or plywood may be used as a cheaper substitute for floorboards when laying the subfloor of a room. Many new houses are already being built with floors made from such sheet materials. Plywood is dimensionally stable so makes an ideal base for other floor coverings such as laminated floors and tiles. Whilst it is possible to lay chipboard and ply over existing flooring, bear in mind that this could make access to underneath the floor difficult in the future.

floor finishes

64

tools for the job

tape measure & pencil
cordless drill/driver
hammer
prybar
panel saw or circular saw
carpenter's square
nail punch

chipboard floors

Flooring grade chipboard is generally 18mm (11/16in) thick and comes in sheets 2.4m x 600mm (7ft 10½in x 2ft). Tongue and groove joints provide extra support to the edges. Larger sheets makes it much quicker to lay than standard timber floorboards.

1 Chipboard floors are most likely to be fitted directly to joists. Lay one or two boards down without fixing them to walk around on.

2 Lay the first board at right angles to the run of the joists, starting in one corner. Ensure that the board is placed with the tongue facing away from the wall, and note that all boards should be laid printed side down.

3 Screw or nail the board in place. Screws should be 25mm (1in) longer than the flooring thickness, so a floor 18mm (11/16in) thick will require 32mm (1⅜in) screws. Drive these in at 200mm (8in) centres. Make fixings no closer than 50mm (2in) to any edge.

4 Run a bead of PVA adhesive into the end groove of the next board and push this up to the first board. Endure the joint is tight with no gaps showing on the face where the two boards meet. If hand pressure alone is not enough, tap the end of the board with a hammer. Insert a scrap of wood between the hammer and board to avoid damaging the tongue.

5 Carry on till one row is finished then start on the next. If the last board of the first row was cut to length then start from this end on the second row in order to stagger joints. Do not worry if joints do not occur on joists as the tongues provide support.

6 Cut the last boards to width 1cm (½in) less than the overall measurement. Run glue into the groove of each board and place them onto the joists tight against the wall. Force the board onto the tongue of the next board with a prybar.

plywood floors

Very popular in the USA, plywood is often used as a quick method of covering a floor. it provides a very stable and strong subfloor over which tiles, carpet and almost any other floor covering may be laid. Stronger than chipboard, it is better suited to damp environments and can withstand greater weights being placed upon it. If better quality ply is used it can even be varnished and left without any additional floor covering.

1 Ensure the plywood is laid to best advantage. If sheets are being laid over an existing floor then

where the joints fall will not matter. Where ply is being laid directly onto joists the joints must fall onto a joist. Lay down a few sheets dry, orienting them in different directions to check.

2 Newer houses have joists placed at close spacing. In older houses floors tend to be constructed using joists with a larger section but spaced farther apart. Fit noggings to reinforce ply edges where necessary, providing additional support. Use 75 x 50mm (3 x 2in) timbers on edge cut to fit between the width of the joists. Skew nail on each side, through the top of the nogging and into the side of the joist. Keep the top of the noggings level with the joists.

3 Boards can be fixed down by hammering wire nails into the joists and punching the heads below the surface. Alternatively, by drilling pilot holes and screwing them down, gaining access below the floor will be that much easier. Place screws at 200mm (8in) centres with no screw closer than 15mm (⅝in) to any edge.

4 Fit the remaining boards, maintaining a 2mm (⅛in) gap along all joints to prevent the boards from squeaking and to allow for any slight movement. Cut a couple of pieces of scrap timber 2mm (⅛in) thick and place these between the boards to keep the gap consistent as you fit. It also saves having to keep checking the measurement repeatedly.

5 Replace the skirting if this was removed, or install it now if fitting new skirting. Press it down to the floor as you fix it to the wall but do not insert fixings into the floor. If the skirting was left in situ, install a small quadrant or Scotia moulding to hide the joint between ply and skirting.

laying vinyl tiles ⚒⚒⚒

Vinyl tiles have undergone something of a revival in recent years and are now available in a variety of styles and sizes. Some tiles come with a self-adhesive backing, otherwise they are laid by bedding them into a special adhesive. The quality and longevity of the finished floor will depend on the thoroughness of your preparatory work, so make sure any necessary repairs to the subfloor are carried out before you start to lay your tiles.

tools for the job

tape measure & pencil
hammer or cordless drill/driver
jigsaw or padsaw
chalk lines
carpenter's square
serrated adhesive trowel
hot air gun or hair-drier
trimming knife
vinyl roller
wallpaper roller

1 Vinyl tiles are ideal for laying on concrete and hardboard, but cannot be laid on floorboards. If you have floorboards, cover them over with hardboard or ply before laying vinyl. Cut around any pipes or other obstructions. Nail or screw the boards every 150mm (6in) in every direction. Ensure fixings finish below the surface.

2 Jumble up the tiles from several boxes so that slight variations in colour will not be noticeable. Lay a few out for a trial run – you can often vary the look of the floor by alternating how the surface pattern or texture flows.

3 Lay out dry two rows of tiles between opposing walls to form a cross. Leave an even gap between the tile and wall at each end. Mark round the tile at the centre of the cross – this is your key tile.

4 Remove the tiles and, using the key tile marks as a guide, snap a chalk line along the length of the floor. Make sure the line is at right angles to any main doorway or window. You might need to adjust the line a little, but provided the temporary layout was correct then any adjustments will be minimal. With the aid of a large carpenter's square, snap another chalk line at right angles to the first, using the pencil marks as a reference.

5 Spread out a quantity of tile adhesive with a serrated adhesive trowel. Cover an area large enough to lay down the first eight or nine tiles, including the key tile. Work from the intersection of the chalk lines, keeping all the adhesive restricted to one quadrant of the room for the moment. Do not apply the adhesive too thickly – spreading rates are generally given on the tub.

✋ safety advice

Many tile adhesives are petroleum based and give off heavy vapours. Work in a well-ventilated room and extinguish all naked lights.

6 Bed in the key tile, exactly lining up the corners with the right angle of the chalk lines. Then lay tiles adjacent to the key tile, keeping each tile tight to the next. Twist the tiles as you push them into the adhesive – this helps them to bond properly and ensures an even coating of adhesive.

7 Continue laying tiles, one quadrant at a time, wiping away adhesive that squeezes out through the joints. End with full tiles, leaving a gap at the edge of the room.

8 Lay down the last complete tile then align another tile on top so that it touches the wall. Cut through the bottom tile using the top tile as a straightedge. Discard the offcut, then swap the tiles around before gluing.

tips of the trade

Vinyl tiles remain stiff when cold. Warming them with a hair-drier or hot air gun makes the tiles more flexible, easier to cut and improves bonding.

9 To fit the tiles around pipes, start by making a card template, then copy this onto a tile with a chinagraph

pencil and cut out. Cut just one slit down to a pipe hole and spring the tile open as you bed it into the adhesive. Tiles cut in this way should fit perfectly, with little trace of the cut.

10 Immediately you have finished tiling go over the floor with a heavy steel roller to ensure full adhesion. Proceed slowly, moving left to right and up and down the length of the room. Wipe up adhesive that oozes from the joins. Any tiles that the big roller cannot reach, press down with a wallpaper roller.

These tiles have been laid at 90° to each other according to the direction of the 'grain'. For less obvious joins, lay the tiles so that the pattern runs in the same direction.

laying quarry tiles ⟋⟋⟋⟋

Quarry tiles are popular in kitchens, lobbies and other areas where the floor surface needs to be able to endure heavy traffic. They offer superb wear characteristics and require minimal maintenance. However they do have a porous surface and as such it is best not to lay them in bathrooms, where a glazed surface tile would make a better choice.

Quarry tiles must be laid on an absolutely rigid subfloor – concrete screed is ideal. On any other type of subfloor you must put down cement fibreboard first as an underlay. This can be fitted in exactly the same way as for hardboard (see pages 64–5)

tools for the job

safety equipment
tape measure & pencil
string lines
electric drill & mixing paddle
bucket
pasting brush
serrated adhesive trowel
mallet
spirit level
tile & disc cutter
long-nose pliers
rubber grouting float
foam roller

1 It is best to try and limit the amount of cutting needed. Lay the tiles out dry to see how best to arrange them in order to minimize cutting. Then lay out the guidelines as described for vinyl tiles on page 68.

2 Mix up the mortar using an electric drill fitted with a mixing paddle, at slow speed to avoid spills and splashes. Leave it to stand for ten minutes so the air bubbles disperse.

3 Damp down the subfloor with water, but do not soak. This prevents all the moisture being sucked from the mortar as it is spread out. Dip a wallpaper pasting brush into a bucket and flick the water at the floor, covering one square metre at a time.

4 Starting at the intersection of the reference grid, use a serrated trowel to spread out enough mortar to lay a square of nine tiles. Any more than this and the mortar may 'go off' before you are able to bed the tiles in.

5 Push the tiles into the mortar with a gentle twisting motion. Make sure they stay aligned with the reference marks. Place plastic tile spacers at the corner of each tile to keep the joints even. These come in different sizes so make sure you have the correct spacers for the type of tile. As a general guide, the thicker the tile the bigger the spacer.

6 When you have laid the first nine tiles place a spirit level across the surface in different directions. Tap any tiles that are slightly high with a soft rubber mallet. Spread more mortar and lay the next block of nine tiles in the same way as the first. Work back towards a door opening if possible to avoid walking on freshly bedded tiles.

7 Tiles will inevitably need to be cut. For best results cut with a tile cutter by scoring the surface of the tile and snapping. For slithers and corners use a disc cutter.

8 Before the mortar has fully set remove the tile spacers with long-nose pliers. Be careful not to

dislodge any tiles. If any spacers refuse to come out, wait until the mortar has set and prise them out with a screwdriver.

9 Wait for 24 hours and then grout. Start in one corner of the room and draw the grout across the faces of the tiles with a rubber grouting float. Lift the edge of the float at an angle of about 60° as you move it in a figure of eight shape to ensure an even

spread. Force grout into the joints with the edge of the float. Wipe any excess grout on the tile surface with a damp sponge. Avoid getting the tiles too wet and do not pull out the wet grout by scrubbing along joints.

10 When dry, buff the tiles with a soft clean cloth. Seal the surface and joints against dirt and moisture with the recommended sealer, applying it with a foam roller.

If laid correctly, terracotta quarry tiles produce an extremely impressive appearance, reminiscent of Mediterranean decoration.

fitting carpet

The choice of carpet colours and patterns is virtually limitless so it is easy to coordinate a carpet into the chosen decorative scheme of a room. Carpets made from artificial fibres are now suitable for high traffic areas and rooms once considered inappropriate, such as bathrooms and kitchens. Often considered a professional job, carpet laying can in fact be undertaken by a skilled amateur.

Before installing carpet, you will need to estimate the quantity of carpet you need and also the amount of gripper and underlay (see pages 38–9). Carpet and underlay are usually sold by the square metre, although it is still made in widths of 12 and 15ft (3.7 and 4.6m). Gripper has different length pins for different depths of carpet pile, so seek your supplier's advice. Carpet comes in different weights – the heavier the weight, the greater the wear.

tools for the job

tape measure & pencil
secateurs or handsaw
hammer
sealant gun
trimming knife
staple tacker
protective gloves
knee kicker
edge trimmer
bolster chisel
screwdriver

1 Fit gripper all the way around the room. Cut strips to length as necessary with secateurs or a small handsaw. On chipboard and wooden floors, nail it down ensuring that the slanted gripper pins point towards the wall. Leave a gap two-thirds the thickness of the carpet between the back of the gripper and the wall.

safety advice

The pins on gripper are extremely sharp – always wear gloves and safety glasses when handling and cutting it.

tips of the trade

To ensure you fit gripper the correct distance from the wall, make a spacer two-thirds the thickness of the carpet and use this when nailing it down.

2 On hard floors such as concrete use a special adhesive designed for sticking down gripper. Work fast as the adhesive generally only stays workable for ten minutes.

3 Special gripper strips, often called napplocks, are fitted at doorways for a neat appearance. Nail the strip to the floor so that it will be covered completely by the bottom of the door when it is closed.

4 Cover the floor inside the gripper with underfelt, cutting to fit with a craft knife. Leave no gaps but do not overlap, as this will cause an unsightly bulge. Fix the underfelt to the subfloor using a staple tacker.

5 Lay the carpet with the napp sloping away from the main source of light. Trim off excess with the trimming knife leaving 150mm (6in) turned up the wall at each edge.

tips of the trade

The 'napp' of a carpet refers to the way the pile slopes. Make sure that the napp all faces the same way when two pieces are joined together.

6 Press the carpet onto the gripper along the straightest wall with the ball of your hand. Wear gloves to avoid friction burns.

7 Position a knee kicker about 150mm (6in) from the opposite wall and kick the carpet forward with your knee so that it is stretched and held by the gripper. Stretch out the whole width of the carpet.

8 Cut the carpet to size with a carpet edge trimmer. Use the trimming knife to get into the corners of the room. Stretch and fit the carpet to the other wall in the same manner.

9 Force down the edge of the carpet between the gripper and the wall/skirting board with a bolster

chisel. Hand pressure is usually fine, but if the gripper is tight to the wall you may have to tap the chisel.

10 To fit carpet around pipes and other obstructions, cut a slit in the carpet the distance from the wall to the obstruction with a trimming knife, then make small cuts across the edges of the slit. Use a screwdriver to tuck the carpet down around the pipe for a neat finish. Unless the pipe is larger than about 20mm (¾in) it is unlikely that you will have to cut out a circle of carpet.

Carpet can add colour and warmth to a room. Deep pile carpets are the most luxurious, but more hardwearing varieties are available where durability is important.

finishing touches

It is easy to overlook the final details once the main part of the job has been completed, but in many ways the finishing touches are the most important. They put the seal on the completed job and integrate the new work into the old. Although most finishing touches are minor details, those left unfinished will blemish an otherwise perfect job.

skirting boards

Skirting boards are lengths of decorative moulding made from solid timber or MDF that are fixed along the edges of a room to protect the base of a wall from bashes and provide a neat finish to the floor area. For exposed floorboards and timber laminate floors it is particularly important to fit skirting to conceal any expansion gap and generally to tie the scheme together and make the job look complete. With timber and laminate you should aim to match skirting to the type and finish of the wood for the flooring. For less prominent edging quadrant or Scotia moulding can be fixed instead of skirting board.

RIGHT *Painting provides an opportunity to let your creative side show. Here a highly original effect has been created by painting floorboards in a trompe l'oeil tiling pattern.*

sanding & varnishing

Whether renovating older floorboards, removing a floor covering to expose the floorboards underneath or laying entirely new boards, traditional wooden flooring should be given a thorough sanding to clean it up and then varnished, stained or painted and varnished to seal it against stains. Sanding an entire floor can seem quite a daunting task but by hiring electric floor sanders the job is made much easier. If you are employing electric sanders follow the professional method demonstrated in the diagram on page 124. Once you have sanded the floor, it is important to apply a varnish coat as soon as possible. If the finishing

LEFT *Skirting gives a decorative finish to a floor and can help to seal the edge of the flooring material in a bathroom – just ensure the wood is properly protected against damp. Torus skirting is shown here but for a less ornate look try ovolo skirting.*

is not attended to, the floor can quickly become marked and scuffed, in which case you will find yourself having to sand the whole thing all over again. Make sure you do not let the finishing part of the project drag on and on. Apply any finish as soon as is practicable. Not only will this give the work a polished appearance, but it will also afford a good deal of protection to the flooring material.

carpet cut-outs

When installing fitted carpet, it is a good idea to order more than you actually require to cover the overall floor surface. This extra quantity can be saved and used to replace worn spots, as natural wear and tear takes it toll over time. If these replacement sections are carefully installed the seams will eventually blend in with the older carpeting. If you have an open fire, it is wise to custom-cut a piece of the carpet to lay in front of the fireplace, the edges of which can be whipped to create a more finished look. This extra section will protect the main carpet from

RIGHT *A vital finishing touch in bathrooms is to apply sealant around the edges of the floor. This will help to prevent damp penetrating underneath and causing future damage.*

BELOW *Where rooms have different carpets, fitting an edging strip at the doorway will cover the join.*

spits of fire and is far easier and less expensive to replace. Planning ahead to make this small initial investment will prevent you from having to tear up and replace parts of the fitted carpet later on. For those with an adventurous spirit, tiling may be combined with a carpeting project. Cut-outs can be made on each stair and on the landings in a variety of patterns. Decorative tiles may then be installed in the openings in the places where carpeting is prone to wear. This project can be undertaken when carpeting is originally laid, or later when the carpet begins to wear, which will help to avoid the cost of replacing the entire stairway carpet.

THRESHOLD STRIPS

To finish off the detail at door openings where one floor covering joins another, install a threshold strip of either wood or metal. This strip protects vulnerable edges and leads the eye seamlessly from one room to the next.

SEALING FLOORS

In bathrooms and kitchens it is a good idea to run a bead of clear silicone sealant around the edge of the room to prevent water from finding its way under the floor. A new floor in a bathroom or kitchen can also make wall tiles look far from fresh. Consider regrouting or bleaching grouted joints to brighten them up.

stair types
& construction

Stairs all perform the same basic function of allowing access between different levels of a building, but that does not mean all stairs are alike. There are numerous methods of construction and staircase styles, but by far the most common method of construction is with timber. Easier and cheaper to build than any other type of stairs, a timber staircase will last for many years if well constructed. Concrete and cast iron may also be used in stair construction, or a combination of these materials. Whatever type of staircase you have, it will often be the first thing people see when they visit your home, so it is important to make the most of it. Understanding different types and how they are constructed will give you a better insight into what can be achieved with any staircase, however grand or small.

A stained or hardwood staircase can look
quite formal. If your hall is not as large as this,
paint handrails and balusters in a light colour.

timber stairs

In private homes the majority of staircases are manufactured from timber. If the stairs are in particularly bad shape then replacing them entirely is often a more economical option than attempting to repair or refurbish them. With most older stairs you will find the structure is sound but there are just a few creaks. These can be effectively repaired and given a new finish by being sanded and then painted or stained, and when this is combined with a new set of spindles and newel post or panelling under the stairs, a total revamp can be achieved for relatively little cost.

closed tread

Closed tread stairs are the simplest to make and are undoubtedly the most common – most modern houses include a staircase with a single straight flight of stairs of closed tread construction. More traditional closed tread stairs tend to be made from solid timber, but with the invention of relatively inexpensive manufactured building boards, on many modern staircases treads and risers will often be made from MDF or plywood.

Building regulations state that a staircase with over sixteen treads must incorporate a landing. Few domestic staircases are greater then twelve treads but they may still include a landing if the stairs turn a corner.

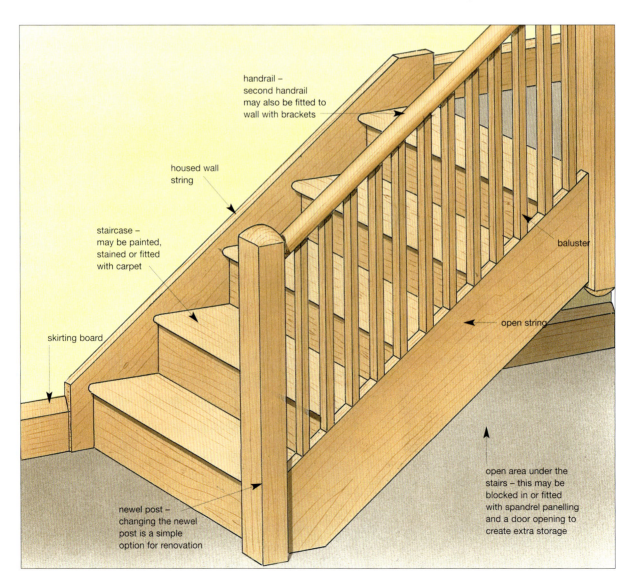

handrail – second handrail may also be fitted to wall with brackets

housed wall string

staircase – may be painted, stained or fitted with carpet

skirting board

newel post – changing the newel post is a simple option for renovation

baluster

open string

open area under the stairs – this may be blocked in or fitted with spandrel panelling and a door opening to create extra storage

Open tread stairs are similar to closed tread stairs except that more of a feature is made of the staircase. Although once very popular, nowadays domestic staircases are seldom built with an open tread construction, partly because of changing trends and fashions and partly because of the increased cost of production. Lacking the support of risers, the treads must be more stoutly constructed to be able to cope with the loads placed upon them without deflecting. For obvious reasons open tread stairs are not usually covered with carpet, but the treads tend to be made of hardwood which can be stained, varnished, polished or painted. The absence of risers mean that these stairs cannot be boxed in with any great success. Indeed, the very idea of the open tread is to allow the eye to see other parts of the room and the structure of the building.

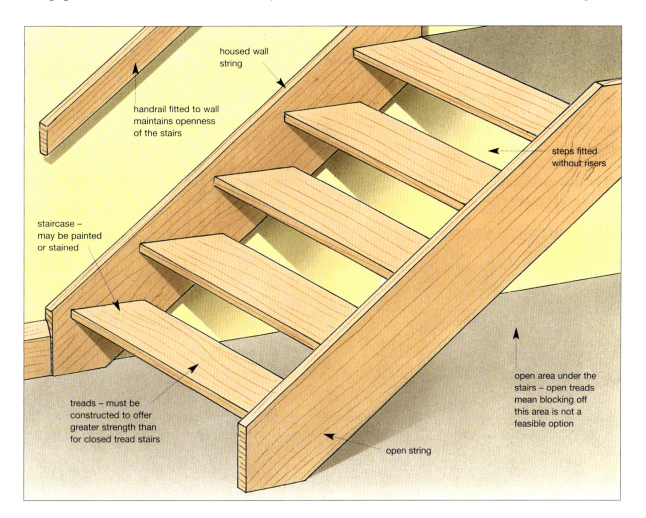

housed wall string

handrail fitted to wall maintains openness of the stairs

steps fitted without risers

staircase – may be painted or stained

treads – must be constructed to offer greater strength than for closed tread stairs

open area under the stairs – open treads mean blocking off this area is not a feasible option

open string

timber stairs

81

CHOOSING TIMBER

Stairs can be so much more than just a means to travel from one level to another. There is a huge range of timbers suitable for stair construction if you are considering installing a new staircase or completely replacing an existing one. You may buy a pre-constructed stairway, or you may choose to have one custom-made.

The cost depends on the type timber you choose. If you select a hardwood timber such as oak, be prepared to pay a premium price. Conversely, softwood timber such as pine will be far more affordable. You can always use cheaper wood or manufactured boards if the stairs are to be painted, but a pine stair will look good stained or varnished.

RENOVATING A STAIRCASE

Another option is to dress up the stairway you already have. Many DIY stores offer stair part kits to transform the look of a staircase. Without touching the treads and risers it is possible to remove the existing newel, balusters and handrail, replacing these with something else better suited to your taste and the surrounding decor.

altering a staircase

There can be a variety of reasons for wishing to alter a staircase, and a staircase can be altered in a variety of ways. For example, you might want to fit a balustrade for reasons of safety and appearance, or to convert the area underneath a stairway into a cupboard, or you may have decided that a cosmetic change is all that is needed and would like to paint or stain the stairs a different colour. Before any such projects can be undertaken, you must first check that the basic structure of the staircase is sound and make any necessary repairs. Once you have satisfied that requirement you may proceed on any number of projects for altering the staircase.

Spandrel panelling may be fitted underneath these stairs to create extra storage or closet space for minimal investment.

fitting handrail bolts ✐✐✐✐

Handrail bolts represent the more traditional method for joining together two sections of handrail. Although, to a certain extent, their use has been superseded by other methods, when properly executed handrail bolts remain an unsurpassed joining mechanism. Requiring no glue, they are ideal for joining a straight section of handrail to a curve at the junction of a landing or at the junction between different flights of a staircase.

Joining sections of handrail together using the bolt method requires a high degree of skill, and accuracy is essential for best results both in the marking out and cutting. Therefore this project should only be attempted if you are confident of your abilities, and this is certainly not a job for a beginner. You are unlikely to be able to find handrail bolts in your local general DIY store. These will most probably need to be bought from a specialist hardware retailer.

tools for the job

panel saw

mitre box

tape measure & pencil

square

cordless drill/driver

6mm (⁵/₁₆in) chisel

nail punch

1 Take the two sections of handrail and, using a panel saw, cut the ends to be joined so that they are precisely square. Make the cuts in a mitre box using the right angle cut

guide, then check how the ends butt together. Rest the sections on a flat surface and bring together the two ends. There should be no gaps, and if there are you will need to recut the joints until perfect.

2 Establish a centreline on the flat underside of one handrail section. Draw a neat pencil mark down this line to approximately 100mm (4in) from the cut end.

tips of the trade

A trick for finding the centreline of anything is to measure across at an angle until the measurement is easily divisible by two, then make a pencil mark at this point. This will give the exact centre irrespective of the actual half measurement.

3 Transfer this mark from the underside onto the cut face using a square, continuing the pencil mark until you reach the top surface. Accurately measure up half the height of the handrail and mark on this point square to the guideline.

4 Repeat steps 2 and 3 for the other section of handrail, then briefly put the sections to one side. Now take the handrail bolt and screw both nuts onto either end, screwing them so that a couple of threads are projecting past the nuts at either end. Carefully measure the distance between the inside edge of both nuts, divide this by two and mark the dimension onto the underside of the handrail along the centreline.

5 Drill into the end face of each handrail section at the centre point marked in step 3. Use a drill bit 2mm (¹/₁₆in) larger than the diameter of the bolt and 10mm (½in) deeper than half the overall length of the bolt.

6 Use a 6mm (⁵/₁₆in) chisel to cut a pocket in the underside of one of the handrail sections, into which the square nut will be dropped. Chisel out the timber at the point marked in step 4. Note that the pocket should be on the side of the line furthest from the end of the handrail. Once the pocket is complete, drop the square nut into it, allowing the bolt to poke through the hole and enter the thread.

7 In the same way, cut the pocket for the round serrated nut on the other handrail section. The pocket should be slightly larger to allow the nut to turn on the bolt.

8 Use a small nail punch to tighten the serrated nut so that the two halves of the handrail are pulled up tight. Do not overtighten or you may split the timber. Proving that you have been accurate, the two sections should form a perfect fit.

9 Use a sanding block and abrasive paper to sand across the completed joint in order to blend any slight irregularities. Finally, fit the handrail into position on the stairs. Should the joint open up in the future, gently retighten the serrated nut.

A 'reef' is the section of handrail that goes around a corner and connects one straight section to another. A handrail bolt is ideal for joining these sections together.

installing balusters ⚒

It is often the case that balusters are changed at the same time as the newel posts to alter entirely the look of the stairs. The style of spindles you ultimately go for will depend on personal preference and your budget. You should consider which type of spindles will contribute best to the overall style that you are trying to achieve. Buying the most expensive hardwood balusters could be a waste of money if you are going to end up painting them, when cheaper softwood spindles would have given the same result for less money.

You will need to fit two spacer blocks and two baluster spindles for each stair tread, plus the string capping and a new handrail if this is being replaced at the same time (see also pages 90–3). All the parts should be available from good DIY stores.

tools for the job

tape measure & pencil

handsaw

nail punch

hammer

spirit level

sliding bevel

sanding block

1 Place the capping that houses the bottom of the balusters on top of the string, and slide it down until it touches the newel. Holding a scrap of timber against the newel, mark then cut the necessary bevel.

2 Repeat the process at the top of the stairs, then nail through the capping into the top of the string, setting the nails below the surface of the capping with a nail punch.

3 Mark a plumb line with a spirit level on both the handrail and string capping. The position of this line does not matter as it is simply a guideline to help you mark the length of the balusters. Draw equivalent lines across the top of the capping and underside of the handrail.

4 Use two lengths of thin batten to act as a pinch rod for measuring the height of the balusters. Hold the two sections together and then slide them apart until they touch the plumb line marks made on the capping and handrail. Tape together the two pieces to preserve the measurement.

5 Hold the pinch rod against one of the balusters and transfer the height measurement. Set a sliding bevel to the angle between the newel post and string capping, and transfer this bevel to the baluster. Note that the top and bottom bevels slope in the same direction.

tips of the trade

Store the balusters indoors for a few days so that they can acclimatize to the temperature and humidity of the house prior to fitting. This will ensure they do not shrink afterwards, which will cause them to rattle.

6 Cut the bevels onto each end of the baluster and then place it between the handrail and capping to check for fit. Hold a spirit level against the baluster when in position to make sure that it is plumb. If you are happy with the fit, use this first baluster as a pattern for cutting all the others.

safety advice

Make sure that the spindles are not spaced too far apart, which could allow a child to fall through.

7 Starting at the bottom of the staircase, nail the first two spacer blocks, one to the underside of the handrail and the other to the string capping. Use a nail punch to set the nail heads below the surface.

8 Add the first baluster, then follow this with the next spacer block, and so on until you reach the top of the stairs. No fixings are made through the balusters

themselves. Only the spacer blocks are fixed in place as these are sufficient to hold the balusters.

9 When all the balusters have been fitted, give them a light rub over with a sanding block and abrasive paper, then apply your chosen finish.

👍

tips of the trade

If you have chosen barley twist-style balusters, make sure that the twists all start in the same position at the bottom. This makes for a neater and more professional appearance.

Combined with a decorative handrail and newel post, balusters provide an ornate finish to a staircase. They also represent a safety option, especially if you have children.

blocking in the underside of a staircase ⚹⚹

In smaller homes it may not be appropriate to fit spandrel panelling underneath a staircase if this would cause a portion of the main living space to be blocked off. You may instead want to consider leaving the side of the stairway open and disguising the architecture and construction details on the underside with the addition of a flat panel. If your needs change or you feel more confident in your DIY abilities, there is always the option to add spandrel panelling at a later date.

Plasterboard is commonly used to form the panel, although it is heavy and difficult to handle, and many other materials will do just as well. For the project demonstrated on these pages the panels have been cut from thin plywood instead. Lightweight and easy-to-handle, working with plywood means it is perfectly feasible for a DIYer of average skill to undertake this project single-handed and easily complete it over a weekend. Timber battens form the framework for fixing the panels, and since these are small and thin it is important to use good quality timber with minimal defects.

tools for the job

tape measure & pencil

handsaw

screwdriver

hammer

nail punch

wallpaper brush & roller

1 Cut small sections of 25 x 25mm (1 x 1in) battens to act as set-backs, against which cross pieces will be fixed at 200mm (8in) centres to form the framework for the panels. You will need to cut two for each cross piece – make a template to save having to measure each individual piece when cutting. When you have cut enough pieces, measure and mark midway between each step the distance these pieces will need to be set back from the edge of the

string to accommodate the cross pieces. Since the cross pieces are cut from the same batten, this will be 25mm (1in). Glue and screw each set-back in the marked positions.

2 Measure and cut sufficient cross pieces to provide supports at 200mm (8in) centres. Fix these into position by skew nailing or screwing through each end at an angle into the set-back sections of batten.

3 Cut 6mm (⁵/₁₆in) ply to fit across the width of the stairs, from string edge to string edge, so that any joints meet on the cross pieces.

4 Mark the centrelines of the cross pieces a little way onto the sides of the strings. Spread wood glue onto the face of each cross piece and fix the panels into position on the strings with 20mm (³/₄in) panel pins. Join up the pencil marks across the face of the panels with a straightedge. These will act as guidelines for fixing panel pins into the cross supports.

tips of the trade

On older stairs where access might be needed later, omit the glue and fix the panels with small screws.

5 Set the pin heads just below the surface of the plywood with a nail punch. Disguise the holes left by the nails by smoothing in enough wood filler so that it sits slightly proud. Leave to dry then sand smooth.

6 Nail on some trim to cover the exposed joints between ply and string. This also helps to cover the slots left by the router for the treads and risers when the stairs were built.

tips of the trade

When fixing delicate trim use veneer pins instead of panel pins, as they are thinner and less obtrusive and require less filler to disguise the nail heads.

7 Finally, decorate the surface of the finished panelling to match or blend with the existing decoration in the room for a unified look. If applying wallpaper as shown, buy a good quality wallpaper to ensure an adequate bond with the plywood.

tips of the trade

If you plan to wallpaper the plywood panelling, it is a good idea to apply a coat of emulsion paint to the side of the panel that will face the back tread of the stairs prior to fixing. This may seem like an unnecessary job as it will never be seen, however, it will prevent the wood from warping and this in turn ensures the panel remains flat and the wallpaper does not peel.

UNDERSTAIRS LIGHTING

If the underside of the stairs could do with some additional illumination, one idea is to fit recessed lights. You will need to run the necessary wiring before you fit the panels. Use a jigsaw to cut the hole into the ply panel as instructed by the manufacturer. Installing electrical lighting is a complicated procedure and you must not take chances with electricity – employ a qualified electrician for wiring up the lights and final connection.

Finished with the appropriate decoration, blocking in both conceals the underside of a staircase and incorporates the stairs more into the overall decor of the room or hall.

painting stairs

Achieving a professional finish when applying paint to stairways and landings can be a difficult process. There are so many little nooks and crannies that the idea of undertaking a complete redecoration can be a daunting prospect. However, by following the correct steps and working methodically to ensure each step has been properly completed before moving on to the next, you can expect superb results.

As with so many projects concerned with achieving a fine decorative finish, careful preparation is the key to success. It is vital to spend sufficient time preparing the stairs so that they are in the right condition for receiving the paint finish. Hence after you have removed old paint, stain or varnish, you will need to carry out any repairs before applying the new finish. See pages 128–33 for how to carry out repairs. Newer stairs that do not have a build up of paint or other finishes can be redecorated after they have been rubbed down with sandpaper.

Aim to apply at least one primer coat, two undercoats and two top coats. One-coat and self-undercoating gloss paints are available, but they are seldom as durable as a correctly applied paint system. If your stairs are older, you may be pleasantly surprised to find that burning or stripping paint off exposes detailing previously lost under layers of old finishes.

safety advice

Many older houses may have been painted with lead-based paints. If you suspect that the staircase has been painted with lead paint, you must limit the amount of dust created. One way to do this is to rub down paintwork with wet-and-dry paper used wet. You should also avoid the use of blow lamps and hot air guns, removing the paint with a proprietary non-caustic paint stripper instead. Modern strippers are far safer than older caustic solutions, nonetheless treat them with respect and follow the manufacturer's guidelines. Always wear thick rubber gloves and goggles to protect your hands and eyes.

tools for the job

duct tape & trimming knife

bucket & sponge

dust mask & goggles

blow lamp or hot air gun

wire wool

orbital sander

tack rags

paintbrushes

sanding block

abrasive paper

clean rags

1 Remove the stair carpet or other flooring material, if fitted. Leave the grippers in place if you intend to refit the carpet, but stick duct tape over the pins to protect hands, feet and knees from injury.

2 Wash down the existing finish with sugar soap, following the manufacturer's recommendations. Do this only if you intend to sand down the paintwork in preparation for the next finish. If you are burning off the paint there is no need to wash down the surfaces.

3 The quickest way to remove thick layers of old paint is to burn them off with the aid of a blow lamp or hot air gun. These may be bought or hired from good tool shops. Apply just enough heat to bubble the paint, then use a paint scraper to scrape it off while still soft.

safety advice

Blow lamps and hot air guns can cause a fire if used carelessly. Keep the blow lamp or gun continuously moving to avoid scorching the wood or starting an accidental fire. Have a fire extinguisher or a bucket of water handy in case of an accident.

4 When you have burnt off as much of the old paint as possible with the blow lamp, use coarse wire wool to remove any remaining paint. This can be dusty work so wear a suitable dust mask.

5 Use an electric sander on larger flat surfaces. Start with 80-grit and finish with 120-grit paper. Work into the corners with paper wrapped around your fingers or a flat stick.

6 Tear thin strips of abrasive cloth and while holding them between the thumb and forefinger in each hand, work them back and forth to clean up circular and barley twist baluster spindles.

7 When all the old paintwork has been completely removed, the next stage is to prepare a dust-free surface to receive the new paint finish. Vacuum the stairs to pick up as much dust as possible, then rub over the surface with a tack rag to remove any remaining dust particles.

tips of the trade

New brushes are prone to shedding hairs, which then tend to stick in the paint and so mar the final finish. To prevent this happening, use the new brush to apply the undercoats so that it gets broken in, then follow that with a thorough cleaning. After the brush has been used and cleaned several times over, any loose bristles will have come out before the top coat is applied.

8 The first stage of the painting process is to brush primer onto the bare wood. It is important to follow the correct sequence for application – first balusters, then the handrail and finally treads and risers.

9 Once the primer coat has dried, proceed to the undercoat. Follow the paint manufacturer's application guidelines, but always apply at least two undercoats. Follow the same application sequence as for the primer coat. Wait for the final coat to dry, then wet down 350 wet-and-dry abrasive paper to rub down the surface. Dry off with a clean rag.

10 The staircase surface is now ready to receive the final paint finish. Brush on the top coat with a good quality bristle brush. Follow the same application sequence used for the primer and undercoats.

repair & renovation

Every home, whatever its age, will need some degree of regular maintenance – the amount will usually depend on how well and how often repairs were carried out in the past. It is well worth taking your time to ensure the job is done effectively, as there is nothing more irritating than having to carry out the same repair for a second time just a few months later. Carrying out repairs will in itself breathe new life into older floors and stairs, but if you also wish to alter the look then this chapter offers several easy renovation ideas.

111

Old floorboards can be made to look good as new by replacing any damaged boards and stripping and varnishing the wood surface.

replacing a section of floorboard ✂✂

Just about every house will include an area of wooden flooring, whether in the form of timber floorboards or manufactured boards such as chipboard. Wooden floors generally require little in the way of maintenance, but there are times when individual boards need attention. For example, you may need to replace a timber floorboard that has split or been irreparably damaged on its surface, or if access is required to pipes underneath the floor then boards may need to be cut out and new ones fitted. Replacing a section of flooring is a relatively straightforward task.

timber floorboards

The procedure for replacing timber floorboards described below applies to boards fitted with a tongue and groove mechanism. These are slightly more difficult to remove and some of the stages mentioned can be omitted if the floor is constructed from straight-edged boards, which makes the job slightly less taxing. In some rooms, especially those that are fairly small, the boards tuck under the skirting along the edges of the room with no intermediate joints. In this case, simply levering up the board in the centre of the room and slipping a scrap of timber underneath will allow you to cut it in half. If you are at all unsure about a section of floorboard then it is wise to replace the whole length.

tools for the job

pipe, joist & cable detector
circular saw
bolster chisel (wide)
square
fine-toothed handsaw
tape measure & pencil
panel saw
cordless drill/driver or hammer

1 Here the board to be replaced is split down the middle. It is unlikely to be split along its entire length, so first inspect the damage to assess whether you can just replace a small section of the board.

2 Identify joist positions, either with the use of a pipe, joist and cable detector or by following the line of nails. Mark with a pencil if any run below the board to be replaced. Locate the joist just beyond the end of the split and mark this too. For safety reasons it is also vital to find out whether any pipes or electric cables run under the boards before cutting.

3 Set a circular saw so that it will cut to a depth of approximately 15mm (⅝in). Run the blade along both sides of the split board to cut through the tongues. If the floor has been constructed using square-edged boards then this step can be omitted.

safety advice

Circular saws are safe if used correctly, but not everyone is comfortable with them. If you are unsure, a floorboard saw (a special handsaw with a curved blade) may be used instead.

4 Insert a wide bolster chisel into the cut side and gently lever up the board. Start near the joint and work your way along the board. Hold up the board with a scrap of timber and draw a line across with a square, ensuring any joint will be over the centreline of the joist. Cut this line with a fine-toothed handsaw.

5 Measure and cut a new section of floorboard to fit neatly into the space left by the broken section. If you are using tongue and groove board you will need to cut off the tongue with a panel saw before fitting.

6 Once the new board has been cut to a precise fit, either nail or screw it in position. You may prefer to use screws if access to the underfloor area is likely to be required at some future date.

chipboard floors

It is highly unlikely that a section of chipboard floor will split in the same way that a timber floorboard might, but you may still encounter situations where a section will need to be replaced. For example, you might have to replace one or more boards after cutting through to gain access to the underfloor services, or you might need to cut out and replace boards that have become unsound due to moisture damage.

tools for the job

tape measure & pencil
circular saw
bolster chisels (wide)
claw hammer
clamps
handsaw
cordless drill/driver

1 Set a circular saw to a 15mm (⁵⁄₈in) depth of cut and saw all around the edge of the board to remove the tongue. Be careful not to cut into adjacent boards.

2 Gently lever up the board using wide bolster chisels. Do not lever in just one position but work all around the perimeter. The nails should come up with the board, otherwise pull them out with a claw hammer.

3 Install noggings between joists to support any board edges that do not join on a joist.

4 Saw off the tongues of the replacement board with a panel saw, so that it will fit into the gap.

5 Finally, fit the new board into the hole and fix it in position. Nails can be used as fixings but it is better to screw the board in place.

tips of the trade

A screwed board will allow easier access to underfloor services in the future, and screwing avoids the heavy vibrations of hammering, which can cause cracks in the ceiling below.

fitting herringbone struts ✂✂

Herringbone struts provide extra stiffness to upper floors in houses. Made from either wood or metal, they serve several purposes. They stop a floor from twisting out of shape, damp down vibration and keep the joists uniformly spaced apart from one another. It is important to fit them properly otherwise they will cause the floor to squeak.

Unless you are constructing an entirely new suspended floor it is unlikely that you will have to completely strut out the floor with herringbone. More often than not you will find that there are just one or two struts loose or missing when the floorboards are lifted. For new floors, fitting herringbone struts is a relatively straightforward job which has been made simpler in recent years with the introduction of ready-made metal struts. Herringbone struts should be fitted to joists prior to the installation of floors or ceilings

safety advice

When fitting herringbone struts there will not be any existing flooring in place. To make the job more safe and easy, lay scaffold boards or temporary flooring across the joists to create a working platform.

wooden struts

tools for the job

tape measure & pencil

chalk lines

pinch rod

sliding bevel

mitresaw

cordless drill/driver

hammer

1 Measure the length of the joists at each end of the room and divide this into three. Snap a chalk line at both points across the bottom of all the joists.

2 Make a pinch rod from two thin strips of wood about 15 x 3mm (⅝ x 3/16in) thick and about 400mm (1ft 4in) long. Use the pinch rod to measure the distance between the top of one joist and bottom of the next joist. Wrap masking tape around the pinch rod to hold it at this setting.

3 Hold the pinch rod diagonally across a piece of 50 x 25mm (2 x 1in) timber and transfer the measurement by marking with a pencil at either end. Set a sliding bevel to a shallow angle and use this to mark the same bevel across the face of the timber at both ends of what will be the strut. Ensure the measurements are correct at this stage as this will act as a template for future struts.

4 After checking for fit, cut the struts using a mitresaw to achieve the bevel – you will need four struts for each joist. Since all bevels are the same, the cut edge of one forms the end cut on the next strut.

tips of the trade

If you have many struts to cut and install it might be cost- and time-effective to hire an electric chop saw. This tool will help you to do the job in half the time.

5 Position the struts where the chalk lines cross each joist and skew nail them between the joists, first drilling pilot holes with the aid of a cordless drill. Leave a small gap between each strut to prevent any squeaking as the floor moves.

👍

tips of the trade

The biggest mistake you can make when installing herringbone struts is to have them touch at the crossing points. This can cause annoying squeaks to develop once the floor is completed. To avoid this problem use a scrap of ply as a guide to maintain an even gap between struts when fixing them into position.

metal struts

Metal struts have now largely taken the place of wooden struts in most new construction. Requiring no cutting, they are faster to fit and can be bought to suit the spacing of floor joists which are typically at 400mm (1ft 4in) 450mm (1ft 6in) or 600mm (2ft) centres.

tools for the job

hammer

chalk line

Set out two chalk lines as described above. Starting at one end of the room, nail through the hole in the top of each strut, using glavanized nails to fix them securely to each joist. Work your way along the length of the room.

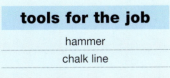Working from the room below bend the struts until they touch the opposite joist. Nail these in position, again with galvanized nails, taking care to maintain a small gap where the struts criss-cross to avoid any possible squeaking.

👍

tips of the trade

Use a set of long-nosed pliers to hold the nails as you get them started into the joist. This will help to protect fingers from accidental hammer blows.

Herringbone struts provide additional support to joists. They can be constructed from either wood or metal, but metal struts are the easiest to fit.

renovating a woodblock floor

Solid woodblock flooring is seldom fitted in houses today as the cost is often prohibitive, but they are relatively common in larger older houses. Resilient and hardwearing when properly laid, they will last for several lifetimes. Major repair is often not required, if it is then this really is a specialist repair best left to the experts. Having said that, it is not beyond the competent DIY enthusiast to replace a few wood blocks or refinish a badly worn floor.

sanding

To sand a woodblock floor effectively you will need to hire specialist machines from tool hire shops. Start with a coarse paper on the sander and finish with a finer grade to remove scratches, after vacuuming the floor surface. A special edging sander is needed to reach those parts that cannot be sanded with the large machine. Sanding can be dirty work and you will almost certainly create a lot of dust. Before you start, remove all furniture and ensure that the floor is clear. Tape up any doors to the rest of the house and open a window to ensure good ventilation. Wear a good quality dust mask and ear defenders when using the sanding machines.

tips of the trade

Any protruding nails or staples will tear the sanding sheets, which are expensive to replace and hire shops often charge extra for the number of sheets used. Examine the entire floor and pull out or punch in anything that could snag on the sanding drum.

sanding procedure

Always turn on the machine tilted back so the drum is off the floor surface. Start at one wall and sand across the room with overlapping passes. If you allow the sander to remain in one spot too long it will cut grooves into the floor.

1 Use floor sander at 45° angle to direction of floorboards, making sweeps across the whole floor.

2 Repeat 45° angle sweep with floor sander in opposite direction.

3 Sand across entire floor surface following direction of floorboards and grain.

4 Use an edging sander to finish the perimeter of the room next to the skirting or wall surface.

5 Use a special corner sander to get tight into corners.

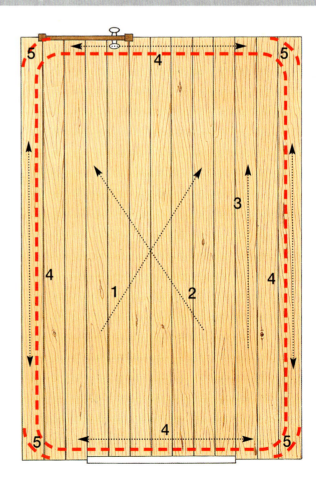

refitting blocks

Blocks are usually laid onto a sand or cement screed with black pitch, but to replace just a few blocks use a ready-mixed latex compound. If blocks are missing your local joinery manufacturer can make replacements, or you might find them in a reclamation yard.

tools for the job

old chisel

paint scraper

old paintbrush

electric sander

1 Remove the loose blocks and scrape off the old pitch from the back of the blocks with an old wood or bolster chisel. Do not use heat as this may set the pitch alight.

2 Spread a layer of latex adhesive into the gap in the floor with a paint scraper, keeping it to a thickness of approximately 4mm ($^3/_{16}$ in).

3 Spread a thin layer of latex on the back of the blocks with an old paintbrush, then immediately lay the blocks onto the wet latex in the floor, following the original pattern of the surrounding blocks. In some cases there will be a tendency for the wood blocks to float on top of the adhesive layer.

4 Take a sheet of polythene and sandwich it between the floor and an offcut of ply, which should be slightly larger than the area of the floor being repaired. Then place several bricks on top of the ply to weigh down the blocks until the adhesive has set.

5 When the adhesive has set, fill any small cracks with a two-part wood filler. Finally, sand the blocks to the same level as the rest of the floor, before finishing to match.

With careful finishing to ensure the refitted blocks match the colour of those surrounding them, the woodblock floor will look as good as new.

painting & varnishing floors

When the budget for home improvement is tight there can be a tendency to leave the floor until you are better able to afford your ideal floor covering. A good way to give a room a finished feel without spending a fortune is by painting or varnishing the floor. As long as the floor is in a reasonable condition, you will be surprised how striking this can look for little cost. If you have a large expanse then including one or two rugs into the finished scheme can soften the effect.

tools for the job

hammer & nail punch
filling knife
electric floor sander
vacuum cleaner
broom
tack rag
paint roller
paintbrushes

varnishing

1 Go over the floor and punch raised nails below the surface. If the floor is screwed down ensure the screws are well below the surface. You may have to withdraw all or some of the screws and recountersink the holes if the heads are any less than 2mm (⅛in) below the surface.

2 Use a wide filling knife and a flexible filler to cover all nail and screw heads. If the floor is to be painted the filler colour will not matter. If varnishing, select a tone that blends in with the surrounding flooring.

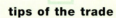

tips of the trade

Almost all fillers change colour when varnish is applied, so it is best to choose a shade slightly lighter than the surrounding timber. Test a discreet section before tackling the whole floor.

3 Once the filler has dried, sand the floor with electrical sanders, cleaning off the excess filler as you go. Follow the method for sanding a wooden floor described on page 124.

4 Vacuum the floor with an industrial cleaner. Use a soft clean broom to dislodge any stubborn dirt and then vacuum once more.

5 Close all windows and doors, then go over the surface with a tack rag to pick up any remaining dirt that might otherwise spoil the finish.

6 Thin down the first coat of varnish by adding about 30% by volume of the recommended thinners. Apply the varnish using a roller with an extension arm. Work back from the main source of light so that you can see those areas that you have missed.

safety advice

Paint and thinners can be dangerous if ingested, especially to children, so never leave opened cans unattended.

7 Let the first coat harden, then apply the next coat without thinning the varnish. Again, use a paint roller, but do keep a paintbrush handy so that you can cut in around the edge of the room and apply varnish to those areas you are unable to reach with the roller. Before you apply the third and final coat, sand any rough spots using fine abrasive paper and wipe up any dust with a clean tack rag. Water-based varnishes in particular will raise the grain to quite an extent, so this light sanding will pay dividends in the final finish.

painting

There are special hardwearing paints designed for floors in garages and workshops. Although only available in a limited range of colours, they do provide excellent coverage and can be used in kitchens, bathrooms and play areas. Emulsion paints are quick drying and will last several years provided they are over-coated with a suitable varnish.

stencilling

A coloured base can be livened up by painting or stencilling a border around the room. Either buy ready-made stencils or cut your own from special stencil paper. Tape the stencil to the floor with masking tape, then stipple a little paint with a stencil brush. Remove the stencil immediately.

applying kiln-dried sand

A simple yet highly effective technique for making the floor surface more safe in bathrooms and kitchens, is to sprinkle a little kiln-dried sand onto wet paint to create a non-slip finish. When the paint has dried, sweep up the excess sand and seal the surface with a coat of varnish.

Dramatic decorative effects are possible when painting a floor. Colourful painted floorboards such as these will make any room feel warmer and brighter.

solving problems with older stairs

Stairs need very little in the way of maintenance and a new staircase should function for years without any major problems. Fortunately, when problems do occur they tend to be relatively minor and simple to resolve, and basic maintenance is usually easy to accomplish. A squeaking stair or wobbly handrail is often more of an irritation than a danger, but small problems such as these should be fixed promptly for if left untreated more extensive repairs will be required.

Almost all problems related to stairs can be fixed with a basic set of tools – the hardest part is often finding the problem. Squeaking stairs are caused by two pieces of timber rubbing against each other, so if a tread makes a noise when you step on it then it is almost certainly due to the tread being split or a loose wedge on the underside. When there are several problems with a staircase, try to work systematically, rectifying each one before moving onto the next.

tips of the trade

Get a helper to walk up and down the stairs while you carefully watch and listen for trouble spots.

tools for the job

tape measure & pencil

panel saw

cordless drill/driver

wooden or plastic mixing stick

hammer

jigsaw

block plane

rubber mallet

syringe

split treads

1 Split treads are common in older stairs and if the stairs are fitted with carpet a sure sign will be a squeaking tread. They can be easily fixed in two different ways. First remove any floor covering to expose the split.

2 If underside of the tread is accessible a patch can be fitted over the split. Cut a piece of plywood 150mm (6in) wide and as long as will comfortably fit between the strings. Coat the piece with wood glue and screw it in position. Make sure the screws are not too long or they will cut through the face of the tread.

3 Epoxy glue is a good alternative when the only access is from above. Scrape out any dust and dirt from the crack then force epoxy into the joint with a wooden or plastic mixing stick. Allow it to harden overnight then sand flush.

safety advice

Many people are sensitive to the components in epoxy resins. Wear disposable gloves or barrier cream to protect your hands.

tips of the trade

Mix epoxy resin with some sawdust for a stiffer mix to make trowelling into wider joints easier. The glue has quite a runny consistency and this will also also prevent it from dripping out.

missing glue blocks

Another major cause of squeaking stairs is missing glue blocks. These triangular blocks reinforce the corner joint between the riser and tread and are fitted to the underside of the staircase (see also page 16). Replace any missing blocks by cutting a piece of timber to the correct size. Coat the replacement block with wood glue, then knock it into into the appropriate channel in the string with a hammer, holding it in position with panel pins until the glue has set.

split or worn nosing

1 To repair a split or worn nosing, use a straightedge to draw a straight line 12mm (⁹/₁₆in) back from the original line of the front edge. Then cut a 45° splay 10cm (4in) in from each end of the tread down to this line, with a panel saw. Having made these initial cuts, remove the rest of the waste timber using a jigsaw.

2 Cut replacement timber, slightly oversize. Glue this in position, holding it with masking tape until the glue dries. When the glue has set, use a block plane and abrasive paper to replicate the original nosing shape.

loose wedge

A gap between tread and string means a loose wedge. Remove the original wedge or cut a new one. Brush wood glue into the groove and tap home.

wobbly newel

1 To tighten a wobbly newel, measure up 50mm (2in) from the base of the newel. Find the centre line and mark where they meet. Drill a 9mm (⁷/₁₆in) hole 12mm (⁹/₁₆in) deep at a 45° angle down to the tread.

2 Continue drilling with a 3mm (¹/₈in) bit from the centre of this hole down as far as the tread. Then insert a 75mm (2¹⁴/₁₆in) number 8 wood screw into the hole and firmly tighten it up. Shape up and glue a small timber pellet to fit the 12mm (⁹/₁₆in) hole and cover the screw head.

loose baluster

To refix a loose baluster, first detach it from the underside of the handrail by tapping it with a soft mallet and pulling it from the mortise in the tread. Clean off all the old glue and brush on new adhesive before renailing it to the underside of the handrail.

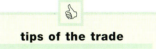

tips of the trade

If the problem requires a repair that involves removing some part of the stair but this cannot be done without extreme difficulty, a good repair can be achieved by squirting epoxy glue into a loose joint with a small syringe.

mending a broken stair tread ⚒⚒⚒

Stairs suffer inevitable wear and tear but they usually remain structurally sound for a very long time. However, if a broken tread is suspected it should be repaired immediately to avoid a potentially serious accident. Replacing a stair tread is an easy enough job for the average DIY enthusiast, but if the fault looks more serious you may need to consult a professional builder.

There are several methods of repairing broken stair treads, but even the simplest will require access to the underside of the stairs. Stairs fitted with spandrel panelling are easy to repair because the underside is readily accessible. For newer stairs that have been blocked in you may have to remove board to gain access and refit it afterwards (see pages 98–9).

(see pages 98–9)

safety advice

When working on stairs, tie a ribbon or a bright piece of tape across the top and bottom of the staircase to prevent it being used. A nasty accident could occur if someone were to put their foot through where a tread is missing.

tools for the job

tape measure & pencil

panel saw

cordless drill/driver

hacksaw blade

wood chisel

claw hammer

rubber mallet

padsaw

hammer

quick fix

If the stair tread is split along its length a quick repair is to glue and screw a plywood patch to the underside. Cut this from 9mm ($^7/_{16}$in) ply, making it as large as possible to keep it just clear of glue blocks and wedges.

replacing the tread

Two methods are used to join treads to risers. Some stairs employ a simple butt joint reinforced into the riser to hold the tread secure. The other, more common, approach is for the riser to be tongued or housed into the tread. To check which type you have, try to insert a hacksaw blade between the tread and riser joint. If you cannot work it through then you have the latter type of joint, which must be cut before the tread can be removed.

1 Prise off the moulding fitted under the nosing with a wood chisel. Keep the nosing for refitting later. Pull out any nails left behind.

2 From the underside of the stairs use a chisel and mallet to remove any glue blocks fitted into the corner of the joint between tread and string. Do not try to save these as new ones will have to be fitted later.

3 Drill three or four small holes of about 3mm ($^1/_8$in) diameter into the riser and through to the tread joint below the damaged tread – these will enable you to insert the blade of a padsaw. Start making the cut with the padsaw, then when it is long enough use a panel saw to finish off the cut, keeping the blade flat to the underside of the tread. Employ the same procedure to saw through the joint between the tread and the next riser, which you will need to do from

under the stairs. Again, make sure that you keep the saw blade flat on the surface of the stair tread.

4 Chisel out the wedges that hold the tread in place. If your staircase is of the closed string variety, free the tread by giving it a sharp tap with a hammer and block of wood right above and adjacent to the string. With the tread free, drive out to the rear again by tapping the nosing with a block of wood and hammer.

5 If you have an open string staircase the approach is slightly different. Prise off the return moulding on the end of the tread, then remove the balusters by tapping them side ways from the shallow mortises before knocking out the tread from the rear.

6 Cut a replacement tread from timber, using the old tread as a template for the new one. Ensure that the timber has the same dimensions as the existing tread and that the nosing is identical to the original, otherwise it will not fit correctly.

7 Refit the tread following the same procedure for removing it, only in reverse. Cut new wedges and glue blocks, coat these with adhesive, then fit by tapping the wedges firmly home. Finally, replace the balusters and return moulding and Scotia moulding if it was removed earlier.

tips of the trade

If your staircase is old or there is any evidence of infestation or rot, both new and old timber must be treated with a suitable preservative before sealing in the underside of the stairs.

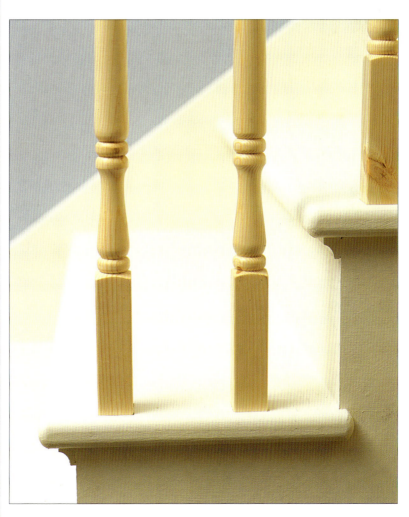

Having made the repair it is a simple matter of returning the new tread to the same finish as the others and the staircase will be good as new.

dealing with squeaking stairs ↗

Irrespective of the quality of their construction, there will inevitably come a time when the treads of a staircase will start to squeak. The main causes of squeaking stairs are simply general wear and tear, coupled with the natural shrinkage and movement of timber, which means that sooner or later almost every staircase made from timber will develop squeaks. In many cases, this is annoying rather than anything to worry over and by spending a little time you should be able to eradicate just about every squeak.

In most cases the best results are obtained if as many of the repairs as possible are made from underneath the stairs. While this is the ideal scenario it is not always a practical option, however many effective smaller repairs can still be carried out from the front. Several different repairs can often be employed to deal with the exact same problem, and most of the options available are demonstrated on these pages.

tools for the job

hammer

cordless drill/driver

saw

screwdriver

wood chisel

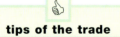

tips of the trade

It will help to identify where repairs are needed if someone else walks slowly up and down the stairs whilst you watch and listen to each step in turn. If you have a cupboard under the stairs you may also be able to find open joints by standing inside with the light off to spot any chinks of light filtering in from outside.

loose tread – nailing

One of the simplest of all repairs, which is ideal if you are unable to gain access to under the stairs, is to nail down through the tread into the riser below. Be careful that the nails do not come through the front of the riser spoiling the appearance. The nails will have better grip if they are inserted in dovetail fashion as shown.

loose tread – screwing

A better method for fixing down a loose tread, again without needing to access under the stairs, is with a row of screws rather than nails. You will first need to drill holes level with the riser just through the surface of the tread and then insert the screws. Use 38mm (1$\frac{7}{16}$in) no. 8 screws and make sure that any heads are

countersunk below the surface of the tread. For the ultimate finish use a screw sink and matching plug cutter. The special drill bit drills the correct size of pilot hole for the screw and cuts a straight counter-bore which sits below the surface. Pellets are then cut from matching timber, glued over the screw head and trimmed off flush.

replacing wedges

A gap between the upper surface of the tread and the string indicates a loose or missing wedge. If loose, remove the wedge from under the stairs, clean off the old adhesive, brush on glue and reposition. If missing or damaged cut a new one from hardwood then glue and reposition.

strengthening joints

To strengthen the joint between an open string and tread, cut a block of wood 35mm (1$\frac{6}{16}$in) square and the width of the tread. Access under the stairs and, at the back of the step in question, screw the wood block into the corner at the joint between tread and string. First coat the block with glue and drill holes for 50mm (2in) no. 8 screws. If you can, get a helper to stand on the tread from above to close up the gap between block and step as you drive the screws home.

loose riser joint

Gluing on a section of a quadrant can sometimes reinforce a loose riser joint at the back of the tread. If the stairs are exposed you may want to give each tread the same treatment to match.

injecting adhesive

You may be able to prise open a joint with a wood chisel and inject adhesive. Clamp the joint until the glue has set. This is effective combined with other repairs, such as replacing glue blocks.

where to insert wedges

Driving in small slip wedges coated with glue is an effective method for tightening joints between tread and riser. Make the wedges about 30mm (1¼in) long tapering from about 3mm (³⁄₁₆in) down to nothing. After the glue has dried use a sharp chisel to trim off the end of any protruding wedges.

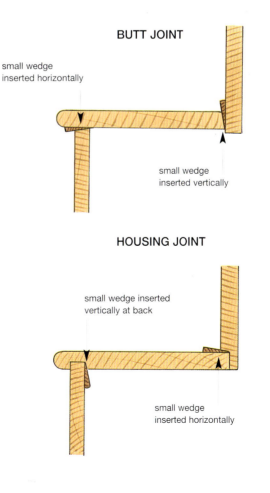

BUTT JOINT

small wedge inserted horizontally

small wedge inserted vertically

MORTISE & TENON JOINT

small wedge inserted vertically at front

small wedge inserted horizontally

HOUSING JOINT

small wedge inserted vertically at back

small wedge inserted horizontally

glossary

Access hatch – hole either round or square cut into a floor to allow access to plumbing or electrical services.

Aggregate – broken stone, pebbles gravel or similar material that forms the largest part of compounds such as concrete and mortar. The finest aggregates are better known as sand. Aggregate is also sometimes referred to as ballast.

Airbrick – special brick built into exterior walls with lots of small holes to allow air to flow into a room or under a wooden floor.

Architrave – decorative strips of moulding fitted around a door frame to create a finish over the joint between frame and wall.

BCO – common abbreviation for Building Control Officer, local authority employee with responsibility for enforcing building regulations.

Baluster – part of a balustrade, the correct term for stair spindles between string and handrail.

Batten – sections of timber 50 x 25mm (2 x 1in) or less in cross section, used for constructing frameworks, etc.

Blinding – sand spread over hardcore layer in concrete floor to prevent the damp-proof membrane being pierced.

Blocking in – the technical way of saying simply 'filling in a space', in the context of this book specifically refers to disguising the construction details of the underside of a staircase with the addition of flat panels of either hardboard or plasterboard.

Bulkhead – partial wall that often hangs over a stairwell or to one side

of the staircase, and which is not directly supported by a floor.

Cavity wall – house wall consisting of two layers, or 'skins', of masonry held together with metal or plastic wall ties, and with a gap (the cavity) – commonly 50mm (2in) wide – between them. The inner wall is usually built with blocks, and the cavity is partially or fully filled with insulating materials.

Cement – binder in powder form that bonds sand or aggregate together to form, respectively, mortar for bricklaying or concrete.

Chipboard – manufactured board used for flooring made of compressed wooden fibres and supplied in sheets. Sheets are normally joined with a tongue and groove mechanism.

Cladding – name given to a material which covers the main structural element below it.

Cleat – small, short length of timber that supports another larger piece.

Closed tread – type of stairs that includes a riser in each step, the opposite to open tread.

Concrete – building material made from cement, sand, aggregate and water that sets to a hard, stone-like mass and is used for floors and subfloors, wall foundations and as cast slabs for laying patios, driveways and the bases for outbuildings.

Condensation – moisture that forms when the air is completely saturated and unable to absorb any more, most

likely to collect on surfaces that are colder than the surroundings, such as cold windows.

DPC – common abbreviation for damp-proof course. An impermeable membrane (formerly slate, now usually plastic) sandwiched between layers of masonry in exterior walls, positioned just above ground level, to prevent damp penetrating to the interior of a house and causing rising damp.

DPM – common abbreviation for damp-proof membrane. A sheet material laid between subfloor and flooring to prevent moisture from rising up through concrete and screeds.

Damp-proof fluid – means of repairing a failed DPC or substitute if none exists, whereby proprietary liquid is injected at numerous points into an exterior wall at the level of a damp-proof course in order to form an impermeable layer.

Datum mark – mark on a wall, or other immovable part, of a known height and from which all other measurements are taken.

Dry rot – type of fungal attack to timber and other building materials. Starts off as minute silky threads covering the timber surface, then changes to what looks like cotton wool balls and finally dark red sponge-like bodies.

Filler – plaster powder used to fill small holes and indentations and to cover nail and screw heads before decorating.

Floor grille – metal cover that is fitted over a hole cut in the floor to allow the passage of air into the room and the area under the floor, can be fixed or with a shutter design.

Formwork – timber boards nailed together to form a temporary mould to support wet concrete until it dries.

Glue block – triangular wooden block fitted at the back of the stairs between tread and riser.

Glue wedge – timber wedge fitted to stairs so that the tread is held tightly into the string.

Gravel – washed river stone typically sieved to a maximum stone diameter of 20mm (³/₄in).

Gripper – wooden strips with nails sticking up to hold in position the traditional type of carpet.

Handrail – rail fixed either to wall or open side of staircase that may be gripped to provide support as you climb and descend the stairs.

Hardcore – layer of concrete floor made up of broken brick, concrete and other masonry rubble laid to build up the level and provide a stable base before the concrete is poured on.

Header – timber around a fire surround to support cut joists.

Herringbone struts – wooden or metal diagonal braces that are attached between joists to prevent movement in floors.

Housing – shallow groove into which another section of timber may be fixed. Of stairs, name for grooves into which treads and risers are fitted.

Joists – large timber or steel beams that support the floor and, in upstairs rooms, the ceiling below.

Joist hanger – metal bracket used to support the ends of floor joists at wall junctions, with varieties specifically designed for attaching to masonry or timber, or some can be built-in.

Joist socket – hole in wall or heavy beam to support joists when joist hangers are not used.

Laminate – flooring material, manufactured using a process whereby a thin layer, usually wood veneer, is bonded to another surface to form one homogenous material.

Landing – the area halfway up a staircase that links different flights of stairs, usually to allow flights to change direction. Term is also commonly used to refer to the area of the upper hallway immediately at the top of a staircase.

Latex – rubber-based material used as a levelling and adhesive compound.

Lath and plaster – a lining for ceilings and stud partition walls in older houses, consisting of plaster applied to closely spaced wooden strips (the laths) that are nailed to the ceiling joists or wall studs.

Mastic – non-setting filler used to seal joints between building components, such as between a window frame and the surrounding masonry. It is also known as caulk.

MDF – common abbreviation for medium-density fibreboard, a manufactured building board made from compressed wood fibres.

Mitred – when two sections of material, often wood, are joined at a right angle, as with architrave at the junction of the top and side of a door frame.

Mortar – mixture of cement, sand and sometimes other additives used for bricklaying and rendering.

Moulding – decoration to the edge of a section of timber.

Napp – slope of the carpet pile.

Napplocks – metal strips with a similar function to gripper rods but used at door openings.

Newel post – main post at the top and bottom of the stairs that supports the handrail.

Noggings – short horizontal timbers fixed between wall studs or ceiling joists to stiffen the structure.

Nosing – the rounded-over edge of a timber tread.

Open tread – type of stairs constructed without risers, opposite of closed tread.

Parquet – flooring composed of wooden blocks arranged in a geometric pattern, another name for a woodblock floor.

Penetrating damp – moisture entering a building through some defect in its structure and waterproofing.

Pile – short tufts of material that actually form the carpet layer, can be plain or patterned.

Pilot hole – a small hole allowing a nail or screw to start into the wood.

Pinch rod – two sticks held between a gap and taped together in order to transfer dimensions from one place to another.

Planning permission – legal permission that must be sought from the local authority to carry out some types of building work.

Plasterboard – a sheet material formed by sandwiching a plaster core between sheets of strong paper. It is used for lining ceilings and stud partition walls.

Plumb – perpendicular, upright.

Plywood – type of manufactured board made from three or more laminations of timber.

Pointing – mortar filling the joints between brickwork. It is formed into different edge profiles using a variety of pointing tools.

PVA (polyvinyl acetate) building adhesive – white liquid used as an adhesive and sealer in building work.

Quarry tiles – hard tiles that have been fired in a kiln, which are used as a floor covering material.

Riser – the upright part of a step that joins two treads together.

Rising damp – moisture entering the building from the ground due to the failure of the damp-proof course in a wall or the damp-proof membrane in a concrete floor.

Rock wool – generic term for insulating material made from mineral fibres.

Skirting board – decorative and protective wooden moulding fitted at the junction between floor and wall.

Spandrel panelling – special panels to fill in the triangular space immediately under a staircase.

Spindles – usually rounded wooden poles that fill the gap between the handrail and string.

Stain – oil- or water-based chemical for changing the colour of wood.

String – part of the staircase structure that supports the ends of the treads and risers (if fitted).

Stud – wooden uprights used in the construction of a wall framework.

Stud wall – wall consisting of wooden studs and covered in plasterboard, used for partition walls in houses and finished with plaster or dry lined.

Subfloor – the base floor material beneath a floor covering, usually floorboards, chipboard or concrete.

Suspended floor – a floor that is suspended between walls.

Tamp down – action of applying pressure to compact materials in order to consolidate them together.

Tongue and groove – male and female jointing mechanism often used to join one or more boards together.

Tread – the horizontal part of a step that you walk on as you go up and down a staircase.

Trowel – tool for moving and working materials, usually mortar, concrete and plaster, of varying size.

Vinyl – manufactured plastic used to produce decorative, easy-to-clean floor coverings.

Wall plug – plastic insert fitted into a hole in a wall to take a screw and make a secure fixing.

Wet rot – wood damage from the moisture content being too high, not as serious as dry rot but still leads to the destruction of timber.

Woodblock – constituent section of a parquet floor.

Wood-boring insects – bugs that live on the cellulose found in timber, an infestation of such insects can seriously damage the wood until it becomes structurally unsound.

Wick – action whereby moisture is absorbed into the ends of timber by capillary attraction.

index

panel mouldings, 36
panel pins, 34
panelling:
    faux fielded, 103
    fielded, 103
    plywood, 98–9
    spandrel, 100–3, 137
paper templates, 70
paraffin heaters, 114
parquet, 60, 124–5, 136
payments, 24–5
penetrating damp, 114, 136
percussion drills, 48
pigments, 13
pile, 136
pilot holes, 136
pincers, 29
pinch rods, 96, 122, 136
pipe and wiring detectors, 33,
    54, 120
pipes:
    fitting carpet round, 75
    fitting hardboard round, 119
    heating, 51
    leaking, 115
    marking position, 51
    metal protectors, 50
    tiling around, 69
pipework:
    installing, 50–1
    insulating, 51
pitch, 60, 125
planning, 22–3
    floor tiles, 62–3
    flooring, 38–9
planning permission, 26, 136
plans, scale, 23, 39
plaster, cracks, 112
plasterboard, 48, 136
plasterboard nails, 34
plastic membrane, 13, 36
    disguising, 45
    joining, 44
play areas, floor coverings, 45
pliers, 28
plumb, 136
plumb bobs, 100
plumbing, access, 52–3
plywood flooring, 15, 37, 61,
    137
    laying, 44–5, 64–5
plywood panelling, 98–9
pockets, cutting, 93
pointing, 57, 137
    damaged, 114

polystyrene:
    cutting, 45
    insulation panels, 44
porous bricks, 114
powder-post beetles, 117
power tools, 29
    drills, 48
    mixing paddles, 72
    powerfloats, 30
    routers, 29, 52–3
    safety, 33, 53, 65
    sanders, 29, 30, 31, 106,
    124–5
precautions, 32–3
preparation:
    concrete floors, 44
    laminate floors, 66
    painting stairs, 108
    spandrel panelling, 100
    staining stairs, 106
    vinyl sheet flooring, 70–1
    vinyl tiles, 68
pressure-treated timber, 49
professionals, 6–7, 22, 24–5,
    26–7
    structural engineers, 105
    surveyors, 112
protecting pipework, 50
prybars, 29, 54
punners, 29, 46
pva adhesive, 35, 137
    joining chipboard, 64
    laminate floors, 66

q
quadrant mouldings, 65, 76
quantities and sizes, 38, 64
    carpet, 74
    chipboard, 64
    concrete, 13
    estimating, 23, 38–9
    floor coverings, 39
    joists, 38
quarry tiles, 37, 61, 137
    laying, 72–3
quarter space landings, 86
quotations, 24–5

r
ramped reducer strips, 45
RCDs (residual current circuit
    devices), 33
ready-mixed concrete, 13
reducer strips, 45
reefs, 93

regulations, 26–7, 105
reinforcing bars, 35, 82
reinforcing mesh, 82
rendering, defective, 114
renovation:
    stairs, 81
    woodblock floors, 124–5
residual current circuit devices
    (RCDs), 33
respirator masks, 32
restraint straps, 49
return mouldings, 16
return nosings, 16
right angle drills, 51
risers, 16, 137
    split, 113
rising damp, 114, 137
rock wool, 55, 137
rollers, 29, 31, 69, 71
roofing felt, 14, 49
rope handrails, 91
rot, 46, 56, 116–17
    dry rot, 135
    wet rot, 137
round head nails, 34
'rout-a-bouts', 29, 51, 52–3
routers, 29, 52–3
rules and regulations, 26–7,
    105

s
safety:
    adhesives, 33, 68, 95
    asbestos, 33
    balusters, 87
    blow lamps, 108
    cement, 47
    chopping out bricks, 57
    electric cables, 33, 51, 56
    handrails, 90, 91
    joists, cutting, 50
    ladders, 32
    lead, 33, 108
    paint strippers, 106
    paints, varnishes and stains,
    33, 106
    plywood sheets, cutting, 44
    power tools, 33, 53, 65
    pressure-treated timber, 49
    sanding, 109
    staple guns, 119
    tiles, cutting, 73
    tools, 33
safety gear, 31
safety precautions, 32–3

sand, 37
    levelling, 55
    as non-slip finish, 127
    soundproofing, 54–5
sand blinding, 12, 46, 134
sanders, electric, 29, 106
    floor sanders, 30, 31, 124–5
sanding, 76–7, 107, 108, 109
    handrails, 91
    woodblock floors, 124–5
saws, 28, 29, 120–1
    circular, 65, 120
    floorboard, 120
scale drawings, 23, 39
schedules, 25
Scotia mouldings, 65, 76
screw bolts, 34
screwdrivers, 28
screws and nails, 34–5
sealants, 35
sealing:
    floors, 77
    quarry tiles, 73
    vinyl flooring, 71
sequence of jobs, 22
services, detecting, 33, 54, 56,
    120
set-backs, 98
settlement, 112
sharp sand, 37
sharpening tools, 33
shave hooks, 106
sheet flooring, 15
sheet vinyl, 61, 70–1, 137
shelving systems, 103
shield anchor bolts, 34
shrinkage, floorboards, 112,
    118
silicone carbide paper, 107
sizes and quantities, 38, 64
    carpet, 74
    chipboard, 64
    concrete, 13
    estimating, 38–9
    floor coverings, 39
    joists, 38
skin care, 33
skips, hiring, 23
skirting boards, 36, 76, 137
    cutting, 100
    fitting, 45
    fitting carpet, 75
sliding bevels, 29, 96
slip wedges, 133
smoothing concrete, 47

useful contacts

143

suppliers

The author, photographer and publisher would like to thank the following companies:

Armstrong DLW Floorings Ltd
Centurion Court, Milton Park
Abingdon
Oxfordshire OX14 4RY
Tel. 01235 444010
www.dlw.co.uk
(cushioned floors)

Axminster Power Tools
Axminster Power Tool Centre
Freepost (SWB30746)
Axminster EX13 5ZZ
Tel. 0800 371822
www.axminster.co.uk

Bosch Power Tools
Robert Bosch Ltd
PO Box 98
Uxbridge
Middlesex UB9 5HJ
Tel. 01895 834466
www.bosch.co.uk

Fired Earth
Tel. 01295 814315
www.firedearth.co.uk
(tiles, paint and interior finishes)

HSS Hire Shops
25 Willow Lane
Mitcham
Surrey CR4 4TS
Tel. 0845 7282828
www.hss.com

Laybond Products Ltd
Riverside, Saltney
Chester CH4 8RS
Tel. 01244 674774
www.laybond.com
(flooring adhesives)

LASSCO
(The London Architectural
Salvage & Supply Co.)
Tel. 020 7749 9944
www.lassco.co.uk

Richard Burbidge
Whittington Road
Oswestry
Shropshire SY11 1HZ
Tel. 01691 655131
www.richardburbidge.co.uk
(decorative timber)

Screwfix Direct
Freepost
Yeovil
Somerset BA22 8BF
Tel. 0500 414141
www.screwfix.com
(tools and fixings)

For information on your nearest DIY superstore, contact the following:

B&Q DIY Supercentres
Tel. 0845 3002902
www.diy.com

Dulux Decorator Centres
Tel. 0161 9683000
www.dulux.co.uk

Focus Do It All
Tel. 0800 436436
www.focusdoitall.co.uk

Homebase Ltd
Tel. 020 87847200
www.homebase.co.uk

associations

National Home Improvement Council
Tel. 020 78288230

British Cement Association
Tel. 01344 762676

British Wood Preserving and Damp-proofing Association
Tel. 020 85192588

Builder's Merchants' Federation
Tel. 020 74391753

Building Research Establishment Advisory Service
Tel. 01923 664000

Electrical, Heating and Ventilating Contractors Association
Tel. 020 73134800

Federation of Master Builders
Tel. 020 72427583

Health and Safety Executive
Tel. 0541 545500

Hire Association Europe
Tel. 0121 3777707
equipment hire

Institute of Plumbing
64 Station Lane
Hornchurch
Essex, RM12 6NB
Tel. 01708 472791

The Ready-Mixed Concrete Bureau
Tel. 01494 791050

Royal Institute of British Architects
Tel: 020 75805533

the author

Mark Corke began his career with the BBC, working in both TV and radio. During this time he maintained a strong interest in woodworking and DIY and successfully renovated several houses. Since 1989 he has worked as a freelance journalist specializing in practical subjects, has written several books and makes regular appearances on national TV and radio.

acknowledgements

I would like to thank all those at Murdoch Books especially Iain MacGregor for his support and professionalism throughout. Special thanks and love to Rita Barry who poured oil on troubled water in times of stress and who had the faith and encouragement that helped see this book through to completion.
Finally thanks to Simon Gilham for interpreting my rough sketches and garbled notes and ending up with the requisite photographs. The Publisher would like to give special thanks to Armstrong DLW, Axminster Power Tools, Fired Earth, Junckers and Richard Burbidge Floors and Stairs.

First published in 2002 by Murdoch Books UK Ltd
Copyright© 2002 Murdoch Books UK Ltd

ISBN 1 85391 969 1
A catalogue record for this book is available from the British Library.

All photography by Simon Gilham and copyright Murdoch Books UK Ltd except: p42 left Armitage Shanks; p8 bottom, pp10–11, pp58–9 and p63 left Armstrong DLW; p31 top right Axminster Power Tools; p7, p21 left and top right, pp78–9, p86, pp88–9 and p93 bottom right Richard Burbidge; p20 left, p42 right, p43 right and p63 right Fired Earth; p43 top right and left Ideal-Standard; p6, pp18–19, p20 right, p21 middle right, pp110–11 and p134 Junckers; p76 right, p77 right, pp104–5 and pp135–7 Ray Main; p62 left MFI (Hygena); p30 left, pp114–15 and pp116–17 Rentokil; p13, p23 left, p25, p27 and p62 right Tim Ridley and Step Editions; p84 and p87 Elizabeth Whiting Associates.

Commissioning Editor: Iain MacGregor
Series Editor: Alastair Laing
Designer: Shahid Mahmood
Design Concept: Laura Cullen
Managing Editor: Anna Osborn

Design Manager: Helen Taylor
Photo Librarian: Bobbie Leah
Photographer: Simon Gilham
Set Builder: John Ireland
Illustrations: Mike Badrocke

CEO: Robert Oerton
Publisher: Catie Ziller
Production Manager: Lucy Byrne
International Sales Director: Kevin Lagden

Colour separation by Colourscan, Singapore
Printed in Singapore by Tien Wah Press

Murdoch Books UK Ltd
Ferry House, 51–57 Lacy Road, Putney
London, SW15 1PR, UK
Tel: +44 (0)20 8355 1480
Fax: +44 (0)20 8355 1499
Murdoch Books UK Ltd is a subsidiary of
Murdoch Magazines Pty Ltd.

UK Distribution
Macmillan Distribution Ltd
Houndsmills, Brunell Road
Basingstoke, Hampshire, RG1 6XS, UK
Tel: +44 (0) 1256 302 707
Fax: +44 (0) 1256 351 437
http://www.macmillan-mdl.co.uk

Murdoch Books®
GPO Box 1203
Sydney, NSW 1045, Australia
Tel: +61 (0)2 8220 2000
Fax: +61 (0)2 8220 2020
Murdoch Books® is a trademark of
Murdoch Magazines Pty Ltd.